NKRUMAH'S LEGACY AND AFRICA'S TRIPLE HERITAGE

D0872857

NKRUMAH'S LEGACY AND AFRICA'S TRIPLE HERITAGE BETWEEN GLOBALIZATION AND COUNTER TERRORISM

ALI A. MAZRUI

Director, Institute of Global Cultural Studies and Albert Schweitzer Professor in the Humanities, Binghamton University, State University of New York at Binghamton, New York, USA.

Albert Luthuli Professor-at-Large, University of Jos, Jos, Nigeria.

Andrew D. White Professor-at-Large Emeritus and Senior Scholar in Africana Studies, Cornell University, Ithaca, New York, USA.

Chair, Centre for the Study of Islam and Democracy, Washington DC, USA

Chancellor, Jomo Kenyatta University of Agriculture and Technology, Thike and Nairobi, Kenya

2002 Series of Aggrey-Frazer-Guggisberg Memorial Lectures delivered at the University of Ghana on March 11–13, 2002

GHANA UNIVERSITIES PRESS
ACCRA
2004

Published for the
UNIVERSITY OF GHANA
Legon, Ghana
by
Ghana Universities Press
P. O. Box GP 4219
Accra, Ghana

Tel. 233 (021) 513401, 513383
Fax: 233 ()21) 513402
e-mail: ghanauniversitiespress@yahoo.com

PRODUCED IN GHANA
Typeset by Ghana Universities Press, Accra
Printed by SuperTrade Complex Ltd, Accra

CONTENTS

PREFACE

About twenty years ago, I offered to speak about Kwame Nkrumah at the University of Ghana, Legon. That offer was for the occasion which was special for commemorating Ghana's independence. I thought, at the time, that it would be especially appropriate to lecture on Nkrumah's impact on Africa and his contribution to Pan-Africanism.

You can imagine my astonishment when the Vice-Chancellor at the time wrote to say that a series of lectures on Nkrumah on such an occasion would be politically devisive, rather than historically celebratory. A quarter of a century after Ghana's independence and ten years after Nkrumah's death, Ghana's founder president continued to have passionate and uncompromising critics at home at that time. In the end, those particular Distinguished Lectures at the University of Ghana by Ali Mazrui were never delivered.

It is now two decades later. Some of the healing has taken place concerning Ghanaian responses to Kwame Nkrumah. The name of Nkrumah still evokes emotions one way or the other, but at least we are now able to come to terms with his significance for both Ghana and Africa.

This monograph is a revised version of the 2002 series of Aggrey-Frazer-Guggisberg Memorial Lectures I delivered at the University of Ghana, Legon on March 11–13, 2002 under the general theme *Nkrumah's Legacy and Africa's Triple Heritage: The Shadows of Globalization and Counter-terrorism.*

In the first lecture, which I delivered on March 11, 2002 under the Chairmanship of Professor Ivan Addae Mensah, Vice-Chancellor of the University of Ghana, Legon, I explored globalization as the product of four engines, religion, technology, economy and empire. Globalization, I postulated, could be positive or negative, depending upon the values it realized. I also introduced Kwame Nkrumah's concept of *consciencism* as a convergence of three civilizations: Africanity, Islam and Western Culture. I renamed this convergence *Africa's Triple Heritage.*

The second lecture which I delivered on March 12, 2002, was Chaired by Professor E. A. Obeng, Vice-Chancellor of the University of Cape Coast, Cape Coast. In this second lecture, I took the concept of globalization beyond Africa itself in terms of the questions: Is there such a thing as *Global Africa*?

Has the Black experience itself been globalized — with Ghana as a major actor in that globalization? And how does all this relate to the shadow of terrorism and counter-terrorism?

I delivered the third lecture on March 13, 2002 under the Chairmanship of Professor Akilagpa Sawyerr former Vice-Chancellor of the University of Ghana, Legon and Director of Research of the Association of African Universities, Accra. While the first two lectures emphasized the shadows of globalization and counter-terrorism, the third and last lecture was out of the shadows and more so with some of the key personalities of Africa's anti-colonial history. Indeed, I examined how Africa sought to be out of the shadows and in quest of an empowered and constructive role in a global order.

I am grateful to the University of Ghana for giving me the honour to deliver the 2002 series of the Aggrey-Frazer-Guggisberg Memorial Lectures, and to Professor Ivan Addae-Mensah, Professor E. A. Obeng and Professor Akilagpa Sawyerr for Chairing the first, second and third lectures respectively.

Binghamton, New York, USA   ALI A. MAZRUI
July, 2002

NKRUMAHISM IN THE SHADOW OF GLOBALIZATION

1.1 Between Globalization and the Triple Heritage

In this essay, we deal with globalization as both a positive and negative force.[1] Globalization is positive when it enhances human communication, improves levels of human productivity, enhances our awareness of being inhabitants of a fragile planet, and facilitates empathy between societies across vast distances. Globalization is negative when it allows itself to be handmaiden to ruthless capitalism, increases the danger of warfare by remote control, deepens the divide between the haves and have-nots, and accelerates damage to our environment.

Four forces have been major engines of globalization across the generations — religion, technology, economy and empire. Kwame Nkrumah flirted early with religion and had once even considered training for the priesthood. It was out of his fascination with religion that Nkrumah's concept of **consciencism** was born.[2] Through **consciencism**, Nkrumah saw Africa as a product of three spiritual forces: the force of Africanity and indigenous African religions; secondly, the force of Islam and Islamic culture; and thirdly, the force of what Nkrumah called "Euro-Christianity" — Westernism secular and religious.

Many years later, I gave this configuration of three civilizations in Africa a different name from what Nkrumah had given it. I named the triad of civilization: **"a triple heritage"**. When Gamel Nkrumah saw my television series *The Africans: A Triple Heritage* (BBC & PBS, 1986), he asked me once in what sense my concept of Africa's triple heritage was different from his father's consciencism.[3] I replied to Gamel that on this issue of three civilizations converging on Africa, I had three great teachers: one was Edward Blyden who wrote *Christianity, Islam and the Negro Race* in the 19th Century;[4] the second great teacher was Kwame Nkrumah. My third great teacher was my own life. When I was growing up in Mombasa, Kenya, I crossed those three civilizations several times every twenty-four hours. I was getting Westernized at school, Islamized at home and at the mosque, and Africanized at home and in the streets. I crossed and recrossed the borders of the triple heritage every single day. I was myself a triple heritage in the making.

It is not often realized that Africa has more Muslims than any Arab country, and that Africa is probably the first continent to have a Muslim majority.[5] The three civilizations differ in weight from country to country. I have done nine hours of television about the triple heritage, and written a book about it. What is different about these three essays is that I relate the triple heritage to **Nkrumahism**, to **globalization** and to the emerging era of **counter-terrorism**.

The second engine of globalization after religion has been technology. Kwame Nkrumah was eager to push technology forward as motor for Ghana's development. The building of the Akosombo Dam had grand ideas behind it about the electrification of Ghana's countryside.[6] Nkrumah's configuration of the project of a nuclear reactor in Ghana was an assertion of Africa's right to enter the nuclear age. Nkrumah insisted that **socialism without science is void.**[7]

The third engine of globalization was economy. Nkrumah was keenly aware of the link between the mini-economies of Africa and the mega-economies of the capitalist world. He was sensitive to the negative side of globalization. He recognized clearly the dependency consequences of Africa's associate status with the European community at the time. He correctly diagnosed that kind of African relationship with the European Economic Community as a form of neo-colonialism.

Nkrumah saw the link between the global economy and global imperialism. Nkrumah's last book while he was still in power was *Neo-colonialism: The Last Stage of Imperialism.*[8] It was a deliberate echo of V.I. Lenin's more famous book *Imperialism: The Last Stage of Capitalism.*[9] In reality, both books identify the negative side of globalization.

Globalization in governance has been leading towards political pluralism and multiparty systems from the former Soviet Union to Zambia, and from Indonesia to Ghana. Different political parties compete to control the power of the central government within each country.

On the other hand, globalization in governance is also leading to dilution of sovereignty within each country and the reduction of the power of the central government. Those European countries which have adopted the EURO as their currency have lost some sovereignty in the arena of monetary control. Regional unification in Europe is reducing the sovereignty of each member.[10]

When one-party states become multiparty systems, more political parties compete for the power of the centre. That is one face of globalization. At the same time, regional unification reduces the power of each **national** government which is another face of globalization.

Where does the legacy of Kwame Nkrumah fit into this? And where does the legacy of the triple heritage come in? Nkrumah's idea ran **counter** to globalization in his views against political pluralism and in favor of the one-party state. However, Nkrumah's ideas ran **ahead** of globalization in his views of continental unification and regional integration.

Nkrumah's philosophy ran counter to history in his policies concerning Ghana. Nkrumah's philosophy was ahead of history in his policies concerning Africa. That is why I reached the conclusion as far back as 1966 that although Kwame Nkrumah was a great African, he fell short of becoming a great Ghanaian.

Nkrumah's greatest bequest to Africa was the agenda of continental unification. No one else has made the case for continental integration more forcefully, or with a greater sense of drama than Nkrumah. Although most African leaders regard the whole idea of a United States of Africa as wholly unattainable in the foreseeable future, Nkrumah, even after death, has kept the debate alive through his books and through the continuing influence of his ideas.[11]

But we must pause here and remind ourselves of the great paradox about Kwame Nkrumah. Although he was one of Africa's greatest sons, Nkrumah was not one of Ghana's greatest servants.

Nkrumah stood for **single-party state** and the **single-state continent**. His dream of trying to create "one-Africa by abolishing separate states" was an inspiration. His policy of trying to "create one Ghana by abolishing separate political parties" was usurpation. Let us first address the negative side of Kwame Nkrumah before we return to his enduring significance as a prophet of Pan-Africanism.

1.2 Between the Single-Party State and the Single-State Continent

The 21st century may be the era when Africans revive the virtues of Pan-Africanism and attempt to bury more permanently the vices of the one-party state. By a strange twist of destiny, Kwame Nkrumah of Ghana was both the hero, who carried the torch of Pan-Africanism, and the villain who started the whole legacy of the one-party state in Africa. Nkrumah was convinced of the need for continental unification leading to the United States of Africa. To that extent, Kwame Nkrumah was ahead of his time. However, Nkrumah was also the man who shackled Ghana with a one- party state, and who utilized the Preventive Detention Act to harass and imprison political opponents. He, even, dismissed the Chief Justice of Ghana for disagreeing with him.To that extent, Kwame Nkrumah started the whole tradition of Black authoritarianism in the post-colonial era. He was the villain of the piece.[12]

It was in 1957 that Ghana gained independence, the first sub-Saharan Black African country to liberate itself from the colonial yoke. Kwame Nkrumah was at the helm. He was soon to become the symbol of some of Africa's deepest aspirations.

I was a graduate student at Columbia University when I first met Kwame Nkrumah in New York. He had come to address the United Nations in 1960 and 1961, and I was invited to one of the parties in his honor. As a young African, my encounter with him captured the very euphoria of the end of colonialism–in spite of the fact that independence for Kenya at that time was still at least two or three years away. In later years, I did meet Nkrumah in Ghana as well, but it was nothing to compare with the historic Pan-African excitement of 1960–61 when over fifteen new African countries became members of the United Nations. Ghana had set the grand precedent of Black African independence.[13]

What went wrong in Ghana after independence? How did this hero of African independence and African unity become the villain of the one-party state and preventive detention?

In a hotly contested article in the 1960s, I described Kwame Nkrumah as "a great African but not a great Ghanaian."[14] In his dedication to Pan-Africanism, he was a hero to our race and to our continent. But, he succumbed to two contradictory tendencies within Ghana at the time — the monarchical tendency, which increasingly turned him into a **royal** figure, on the one hand, and the Leninist tendency towards the vanguard party and the single-party state, on the other. When the monarchical and the Leninist tendencies fused, they basically produced "a Leninist Czar" — a figure using sacred symbolism like *Osagyefo* ("Redeemer") for himself, on the one side, and class-analysis for the rest of the society, on the other. Kwame Nkrumah became increasingly aloof from Ghanaian society–while he bowed to the applause of the rest of Africa at the same time. He became Africa's hero and Ghana's dictator simultaneously.

The question arises whether we should hold Kwame Nkrumah responsible for the origin of the one-party state in Black Africa. As the first Black African country to win independence, Ghana had immense responsibility. And poor Kwame Nkrumah was the beast of burden on whom Africa had piled her weighty hopes. The rest of Africa looked to Nkrumah for a sense of direction. Some of us looked to him for immortal precedents. Was it fair to Nkrumah?

For better or for worse, the two most historically significant Ghanaian leaders so far have been Kwame Nkrumah and Jerry Rawlings.[15] They both had enormous consequences for Ghana. But while Jerry Rawlings started off as a brutal dictator and ended his career as a democrat, Kwame Nkrumah started his career as a democrat and ended it as a dictator.

Three factors led Kwame Nkrumah towards the one-party state. The first factor was the belief that the country was ethnically and regionally too dangerously divided for a multiparty system. Did he genuinely believe that the one-party state was the only way of integrating Asante (Ashanti) into Nkrumah's Ghana? Was the one-party state the antidote to political tribalism?[16]

The second factor which persuaded Nkrumah towards the single-party was the **cultural** argument that African political systems operated on the basis of a consensus. It was, therefore, better to look for manipulated consensus than allow for free dissent.

The third factor that moved Nkrumah towards one-partyism was Leninism. In his years as a student in the United States, Nkrumah acknowledged that the most powerful influences on his mind had been Marx, Marcus Garvey (a Black nationalist) and V. I. Lenin.[17] In reality, the Leninism in Nkrumah outlasted the Garveyism. Indeed, Kwame Nkrumah, after he was overthrown, became more Leninist than ever. But while he was in power in Ghana between 1957 and 1966, pragmatic, cultural and Leninist considerations pushed Nkrumah toward the historical role of setting for Africa the dubious precedents of the one-party state, detention without trial, the destruction of the independency of the judiciary (when Nkrumah dismissed the chief Justice), and the erosion of academic freedom (as Nkrumah attempted to subjugate the University of Ghana at Legon).[18]

Nkrumah's cultural argument in favour of the one-party state became quite popular among subsequent African regimes. Multipartyism was supposed to be alien to African tradition. President Robert Mugabe gave me that doctrine when I interviewed him two years after his country's independence. I am not sure if Comrade Sally Mugabe, the late and dearly missed **Ghanaian** wife of the President, made a contribution to her husband's cultural interpretation of the case for the one-party state. At any rate, Robert Mugabe eloquently made the cultural case for me against the idea of a multi-party Zimbabwe. African indigenous traditions did not institutionalize regular opposition to its own rulers. Mugabe argued, through African eyes, that the concept of a **loyal opposition** was a contradiction in terms. Mugabe has since made such an African opposition increasingly difficult to **remain** loyal.[19]

Julius K. Nyerere even earlier bought Nkrumah's **cultural** case for the one-party state. However, Nyerere's **pragmatic** case was very different from Nkrumah's. While Nkrumah had argued that independent Ghana was too dangerously **divided** to risk a multi party system, Nyerere argued that Tanzania was too happily **united** to afford the "absurdity"of an artificial multiparty system. At independence, the ruling party in Tanzania had virtually swept the board. Why create an artificial opposition? Nyerere's pragmatic argument was, therefore, fundamentally different from that of Kwame Nkrumah's fear of Ghana's disintegration.[20]

Kenya was for so long only partially convinced. That is why Kenya's one-party state was only *de-facto* (in fact) rather than *de-jure* (in law) from 1964 to 1982. Kenya was definitely not converted to Nkrumah's Leninist argument of the vanguard party. But the cultural argument that Africans preferred consensus to competition was for a while sponsored by the ruling party. The pragmatic argument in favour of the one-party state in Kenya arrived after the 1982-attempted coup against President Daniel arap Moi. A constitutional amendment turned Kenya into a *de-jure* one-party state for the first time since independence. Was Kenya, at long last, catching up with Kwame Nkrumah's single-party legacy in its fuller ramifications? Fortunately, the people of Kenya were already restless for a more representative political order. Multiparty politics returned to Kenya after 1992.[21]

1.3 Nkrumah's Ghana and Senghor's Senegal

During Kwame Nkrumah's day, the Francophone foil to Nkrumah's Ghana was supposed to be the Ivory Coast of Felix Houphouët Boigny.

Both countries entered into independence with apparently strong economies; both were led by strong and charismatic political leaders. The big difference between the two countries was supposed to be ideological. Nkrumah had been moving further and further to the left, and had become increasingly alienated from the former imperial power, Great Britain. The Ivory Coast, at the time, appeared to be a model experiment in the free market economy and a hospitable environment for foreign investment and for friendship with the West.[22]

The two leaders, Nkrumah and Houphouët Boigny, are even supposed to have taken a wager between themselves — a bet as to which country would be ahead in a decade or two. The Ivory Coast won the bet at that stage.

But the other West African Francophone country with which Ghana could be compared was Senegal. Both countries were cultural vanguards in an African context. Both had charismatic leaders — Nkrumah in Accra and Léopold Sedar Senghor in Dakar. Both countries had a vision of Pan-Africanism — Nkrumah was committed to the dream of political Pan-Africanism, Senghor was committed to the vision of cultural negritude.[23]

As Aimé Cesair put it:

My Negritude is neither a tower nor a cathedral
It delves into the red flesh of the soil.[24]

Negritude was part of what Senghor called "the Civilization of the Universal" — a new global force.[25]

Both Ghana and Senegal were famous for slave forts important to the self-definition of the African Diaspora — Senegal had Goreë; Ghana had Elmina Castle and Cape Coast. The slave trade was one of the earliest negative forces of globalization.

Both leaders married beyond their ethnic boundaries almost as a political statement — the First Lady of Senegal under Senghor was originally French; the first Lady of Ghana under Nkrumah was originally Egyptian. Inter-racial and inter-continental marriages are manifestations of globalization at the level of personal lives.

Both Nkrumah and Léopold Senghor were also "philosopher-presidents." They were both prolific writers and public intellectuals.

But there were also major differences between Ghana and Senegal. In fact, Senegal and Ghana in some respects defy usual stereotypes. If

I said to my class in the United States that there were two important African countries called "A" and "B" and continued as follows: Country "A" had had many military coups, country "B" has had none; country "A" had executed some former Heads of States, country "B" never has; country "A" has executed judges, country "B" has not; country "A" has often been a dictatorship, country "B" has consistently had a relatively open society. And then I said to my students that one of those countries is primarily Christian, and the other is over 90 per cent Muslim. And I finally asked: Is it the Christian or the Muslim country, which had had military coups, assassinated former presidents, murdered judges, and had had difficulty maintaining a free and open society?

Most of my students in the United States would say that the country with a record of such militarized violence and tyrannical governance must surely be the Muslim one. Yet, you and I know that the fact of the case is that Muslim Senegal has had a better record of political pluralism and civilization supremacy. If political pluralism is one measure of positive globalization, Senegal qualifies. The percentage of Muslims in Senegal is higher than the percentage of Muslims in Egypt. Senegal is 94 per cent Muslim, yet Senegal had a Roman Catholic President for twenty years without riots in the streets calling for *Jihād fī Sabīl Allāh.*[26]

Abdou Diouf succeeded Senghor as a Muslim President — but with a Roman Catholic First Lady — for another twenty years. Then, Diouf was defeated in an election in the year 2000. A President who had been in power for 20 years, and a political party in power for 40 years, graciously accepted defeat in this overwhelmingly Muslim society.

Indeed, Senegalese Muslims were empowering Senegalese Christians at a time when metropolitan France was resenting the arrival of so many Muslims into France. Right-wing groups in France have been known to complain as follows: "We used to go to Africa to build cathedrals. Now North Africans are coming to France to build mosques."

In France, there has been a **cultural conflict** between Islam and French nationalism since the 1970s. In Senegal, there has been **accommodation** between Islam and Senegalese Christianity throughout the post-colonial period.

The percentage of Muslims in France will soon equal the percentage of Christians in Senegal — that is 5 per cent.[27] Yet, while Senegal has already experienced the rule of a Roman Catholic President, it will be many generations before French voters elect a Muslim President of France.

The United States — which separated church from state two centuries ago — has never strayed from the Christian fraternity in its choice of President. American Jews have excelled in almost every field of endeavor, but have so far left the presidency alone. On this issue of the ecumenical presidency, Senegal has been more positively globalized than either France or the United States.

1.4   Nkrumahism *versus* Nasserism

On international solidarity, the Muslim leader Gamal Abdel Nasser of Egypt had a different "triple heritage" from that of Nkrumah. Kwame Nkrumah saw the triple heritage in terms of the convergence of Africanity, Islam and Western culture all over Africa. Gamal Abdel Nasser saw his triple heritage in terms of the convergence of Arabness, Islam and Africanity. For Nasser, the three areas of solidarity were Pan-Arabism, Pan-Islamism and Pan-Africanism. He regarded Western culture as an intrusion into Africa, rather than as a profound element of the soul of Africa. Nkrumah, on the other hand, regarded European versions of Christianity (what he called "Euro-Christianity") as part of new legacy of Africa.[28]

Nkrumah's triple heritage was a better nucleus of Africa's globalization. For Nkrumah, Islam was the cultural wind from the **East** into Africa; European culture and Christianity were the cultural wind from the **West** into Africa; African culture itself was the cultural foundation.

What about winds into Nkrumah's own soul? Within his own soul, Kwame Nkrumah had a different East and West. In fusing religion with secular ideology, Nkrumah proclaimed "I am a non-denominational Christian and a Marxist socialist and I have not found any contradiction in that."[29] Marxism was an ideology of the East; Christianity was the religion of the West. This was globalization at the level of marrying religion to secular ideology.

In fusing socialism with nationalism, Kwame Nkrumah regarded himself as a disciple of both V. I. Lenin (the leader of the Communist revolution in Russia) and Marcus Garvey (the leader of Black nationalist movement in the United States).

This was globalization at the level of fusing international socialism with inter-continental Black nationalism. What was missing in Kwame Nkrumah's own soul was the Islamic factor of his own triple heritage. He himself embodied Africanity and the West. But where was the Islamic factor?

Part of the answer may be sought in Kwame Nkrumah's marriage to the Egyptian Fathia Rizk.[30] He got married to the Arabic language rather than to Islam — thus bringing him closer to Gamal Abdel Nasser's version of the triple heritage.

Abdel Nasser's triple heritage was Arabism, Islam and Africanity. Nkrumah's concept of the triple heritage had never directly included Arabism. It was his marriage to Fathia and the resulting Arabic language of his children, which forged an Arabic component of the cultural soul of Kwame Nkrumah.

Although Nkrumah was Westernized, he was not necessarily pro-Western. A leader can be pro-Western and not Westernized — like King Idris of Libya before Qaddafy or King Ibnu Saud of Saudi Arabia.These were pro-Western Arab leaders who were not themselves westernized.

On the other hand, a leader can be westernized culturally and not pro-Western in policy-orientation or attitude. Today, this group of leaders includes Robert Mugabe. He is substantially westernized in cultural lifestyle, but is far from being pro-Western. Kwame was a little like Robert Mugabe — politically anti-Western but culturally westernized. While Mugabe's anti-Westernism is reducing his relevance as a global leader, however, Kwame Nkrumah's anti-Westernism partially enhanced his globalist credentials. Kwame Nkrumah was taking sides in international conflicts far from the shores of Ghana, whereas Robert Mugabe has been creating conflicts deep **within** the borders of Zimbabwe.

When India and China were engaged in a border conflict, and Harold Macmillan sent military support to India, Nkrumah criticized Macmillan for extending that support. Nkrumah argued that external support to one side or the other would only worsen the situation. When Macmillan argued back that it was right and proper that Britain should come to the aid of another Commonwealth country under military attack, Nkrumah retorted that Commonwealth was not a military alliance.

Long before Israel became so merciless in its treatment of Palestinians, Nkrumah criticized Israel as far back as 1961. Today, African leaders are silent about the brutalization of Palestinians —

although Yassir Arafat was once in the forefront of the fight against apartheid in South Africa. In 1961, Kwame Nkrumah joined the Casablanca group of African states in denouncing Israeli arrogance of power against its Arab neighbours, and Israel as a tool of Western imperialism.

With regard to the American war in Vietnam, Kwame Nkrumah insisted on trying to solve the problem. To his fatal undoing, Nkrumah traveled all the way to Beijing in 1966 seeking a solution to the Vietnamese impasse in Asia. His globalizing ambitions were claiming Africa's right to have a say in the conflicts of others–the way others had often had a say in the conflicts of Africa. In his absence, while he was in Beijing, Kwame Nkrumah was overthrown from power on February 24, 1966.[31] He tried to reach the world — and lost the home front in the process.

1.5 Conclusion

Has the torch of radical Pan-Africanism been passed from Black Africa to Arab Africa? Is Muammar Qaddafy the new voice of militant Pan-Africanism? Like Nkrumah before him, is Qaddafy neglecting his own country while serving the wider "triple heritage"?

In the new millennium, African leaders have started discussing once again concepts like "continental union" and regional integration. In October 2000, I spent three hours with Libyan leader Muammar Qaddafy in his tent in Tripoli discussing Pan-Africanism and Pan-Arabism. The ghost of Kwame Nkrumah was present in that tent in Libya.

Pan-Africanism is a system of values and attitudes, which favor the unity and solidarity of Africans and of people of African ancestry. At its most developed level, Pan-Africanism can amount to an ideology in its own right — a vision of the past, the present and the future and a guide to policy and political action. At another level, Pan-Africanism is an emotional pre-disposition, which identifies with African cultures.[32] Qaddafy was definitely one of the architects of the new African union which is succeeding the Organization of African Unity.

Although leaders like Qaddafy, Julius K. Nyerere and Nelson Mandela have been important in the annals of African unification, Kwame Nkrumah remains the biggest name in the politics of Pan-Africanism in the last one hundred years. No other single individual in this period of history has been more symbolic of the Pan-African dream than Nkrumah. His Pan-African symbolism has continued and will persist long the centenary after his death in Romania in 1971.

A variety of books have been written about Nkrumah's domestic, regional and global concerns. His flirtation with radical socialism, his struggle against imperialism and neo-colonialism, the balance sheet of his policies within Ghana itself have all featured in different works as have debates about his leadership style (charisma, demagoguery, Leninism, Czarist).

By a strange irony, what is perhaps one of the most exhaustive debates on the meaning of Nkrumah which Africa has conducted so far was conducted in the magazine that was published in Uganda and later found asylum in Ghana. The magazine was *Transition,* and the debate started with an article by Ali Mazrui entitled "Nkrumah: The Leninist Czar."[33] Africans, African Americans and others participated in the magazine debate. Kofi Busia, an old antagonist of Nkrumah's and the leader of the civilian wing of Ghanaian politics after the coup, was interviewed by the magazine in relation to the debate. And Nkrumah himself, on receiving a copy of Mazrui's article, wrote through his secretary to *Transition* saying that while admiring the literary skill of Mazrui's analysis, Osagyefo was not provoked enough to reply.

Internally in Uganda, the image of *Transition* as a magazine began to suffer among the more radical members of the Obote government partly as a result of the Nkrumah debate. President Obote actually received letters of protest from Nkrumahists outside Uganda, indignant that his regime should permit a "disparagement" of Nkrumah's achievements. For other reasons, Obote later imprisoned Editor Rajal Neogy and ended the Uganda phase of *Transition* magazine. The magazine that found asylum in Ghana after Nkrumah's fall was edited first by Neogy and later by Wole Sonyinka.

The students in East African colleges in the 1960s also displayed a great interest in analyzing and re-analyzing the meaning of Nkrumah for Africa. In virtually every academic year from 1966 until Nkrumah's death, there was at least one major event concerning Nkrumah. There were debates, lectures, panel discussions and the like. One particularly lively event was a public lecture by the American political scientist, David E. Apter, in January 1969 in the main hall of Makerere on the topic "Kwame Nkrumah: Was He a Charismatic Leader?" The main hall was packed with hundreds of enthusiastic Nkrumahist fans. The American scholar gave one of the most pro-Nkrumah lectures ever heard at Makerere. David Apter, who had known Nkrumah personally and had written about Ghana extensively, captured the Nkrumahist mood of the Makerere crowd in those days. Apter later became a professor at Yale University in the United States.

Apter's address at Makerere was part of a continuing debate about the meaning and significance of Kwame Nkrumah for the African experience. This son of Ghana had had a decisive impact on the Agenda for post-colonial Africa. Africa's relations with the European Economic Community (later European Union), relations between Muslim Africa and non-Muslim Africa, Africa's role in the tensions between East and West, in the Cold War, Africa's struggle for her own liberation and her commitment against what Nkrumah called "Neo-colonialism, the Last Stage of Imperialism" — all these began to take shape in Africa's post-colonial Agenda under the influence of Kwame Nkrumah. But perhaps, his greatest contribution to Africa's Agenda is the doctrine of unity as the basis of all those other African roles, including unity between Black Africa and Arab Africa. Sometimes, his vision of Africa was global — encompassing people of African ancestry everywhere. But, the heartland of Pan-Africanism had to be Africa itself. When Nkrumah said that the two greatest ideological influences on him were V.I. Lenin and the Diaspora Pan-Africanist Marcus Garvey, Nkrumah gave us a glimpse of the parameters of his dream. The Osagyefo's clarion call echoed both Garveyism and Leninism: "Africans of the world, unite! You have nothing to lose but your chains!"

In much of Africa many were listening to that clarion call — others were not. That is the story of this legacy. And the ghost of Nkrumah is still our griot. His legacy is the Odyssey of Pan-Africanism as the new millennium unfolds. He might not have been Ghana's best servant, but he remains one of Africa's greatest sons. Long may he be, not only remembered but debated — in books and ballads, in plays and sonnets, in the media, in the hearts of men and women — and in the lectures at the University of Ghana at Legon.

Amen

NOTES

1. Recent discussions on globalization may be found in Mohammed A. Bamyeh 2000: *The Ends of Globalization*. Minneapolis: University of Minnesota Press; Mark Rupert, 2000: *Ideologies of Globalization: Contending Visions of A New World Order*. London and New York: Routledge); and Colin Hays and David Marsh, 2000: *Demystifying Globalization*. New York: St. Martin's Press in association with Polsis, University of Birmingham, eds.

2. Consult Kwame Nkrumah, 1970: *Consciencism: Philosophy and Ideology of Neo-colonialism*. New York: Monthly Review Press; also see E. G. Addo, 1997: *Kwame Nkrumah: A Case Study of Religion and Politics in Ghana*. Lanham, MD: University Press of America. pp. 153–178.

3. The companion volume to the series is Ali A. Mazrui, 1986: *The Africans: A Triple Heritage*. Boston: Little, Brown.

4. Edward Blyden, 1887: *Christianity, Islam and the Negro Race*. London: W. B. Whittingham.

5. Figures on distributions of Muslim populations by nation state may be found in Azim A. Nanji, 1996. *The Muslim Almanac*. New York, London *et al*: Gale Research. pp. xxix–xxxv.

6. An account of the building of the dam may be found in David Rooney, *Kwame Nkrumah*, 1988: *The Political Kingdom in the Third World* New York: St. Martin's Press, pp. 154–168.

7. Kwame Nkrumah, 1964: *Laying the Foundation Stone of Ghana's Atomic Reactor*. Accra: Government Printer, p.2.

8. Nkrumah's idea of neo-colonialism is explicated in his *Neo-Colonialism: The Last Stage of Capitalism* (New York: International Publishers, 1965).

9. Lenin, V. I. 1939: *Imperialism: The Last Stage of Capitalism*, transl. (New York: International Publishers).

10. For an example contrasting detailed discussions on the impact of the Euro on Britain, see Mark Baimbridge, Brian Burkitt, and Philip Whyman, 2000: *The Impact of the Euro: Debating Britain's Future*. New York, NY: St. Martin's Press, eds.

11. Nkrumah's case for unification of the continent is laid out in his *Africa Must*

Unite London and New York: Heinemann, 1963 and International Publishers, 1972.

12. For more on Nkrumah's tendencies toward authoritarianism, see T. Peter Omari, 1970. *Kwame Nkrumah: The Anatomy of an African Dictatorship*. New York: Africana Publishing Corp,.

13. The transition from colonialism to independence is treated in, for example, Timothy K. Welliver, 1993: *African Nationalism and Independence*. New York: Garland Pub., eds and Prosser Gifford and Wm. Roger Louis, 1988: *Decolonization and African Independence: The Transfers of Power, 1960–1980* New Haven: Yale University Press.

14. This article, entitled "Kwame Nkrumah: the Leninist Czar," appeared in *Transition* (Kampala), Volume 6, Number 26 (1966), pp. 9–17.

15. For a discussion of Rawlings, see Kevin Shillington, 1992: *Ghana and the Rawlings Factor* New York: St. Martin's Press.

16. The Avoidance of Discrimination Bill prohibited ethnic and religious parties; see Nkrumah, *Africa Must Unite*, p.74.

17. See Kwame Nkrumah, 1957: *Ghana: The Autobiography of Kwame Nkrumah* (London and New York: T. H. Nelson, and seventh edition, International Publishers, 1989).

18. Relatedly, see Omari, *Kwame Nkrumah: The Anatomy of an African Dictatorship*, especially pp. 50–78.

19. Consult, for instance, William H. Shaw, 1986: "Towards The One-Party State in Zimbabwe: A Study in African Political Thought," *Journal of Modern African Studies* Volume 24, Number 3: pp. 373–394.

20. An interesting perspective on the trend in Tanzania is laid out in M. Okema, "Tanzania: A Relatively Peaceful Multiparty Debate," *Taamuli* [Tanzania] Volume 3, numbers 1–2, (1992), pp. 1–18.

21. See Jeffrey S. Steeves, 1997: "Re-Democratization in Kenya: "Unbounded Politics" And the Political Trajectory towards National Election," *Journal of Commonwealth & Comparative Politics* Volume 35, Number 3, pp. 27–52.

22. The Ivoirien experiment with capitalism is described in, for example, John Rapley, 1993: *Ivoirien Capitalism: African Entrepreneurs in Côte d'Ivoire* Boulder: L. Rienner Publishers and Davie Lamp, 1988: "A Different Path," *Wilson Quarterly* Volume 12, Number 4 pp. 114–131.

16   Nkrumah's Legacy and Africa's Triple Heritage

23. For a biography, see Janet G. Vaillant, 1990: *Black, French and African: A Life of Léopold Sédar Senghor.* Cambridge, MA: Harvard University Press.

24. These lines are from his poem, "Journal of a Homecoming," (Cahier d'un retour au pays Natal); for commentary, see Gregson Davis, 1997: *Aimé Césaire* Cambridge, New York and Melbourne: Cambridge University Press, pp. 20–61.

25. For some of the seminal works on negritude, see Colette V. Michael, Negritude: 1988. *An Annotated Bibliography.* West Cornwall, CT: Locust Hill Press.

26. According to *The World Guide 1999/2000.* Oxford: New Internationalist Publications Ltd., 2000, p.497, the population of Senegal is 94 per cent, about 5 per cent Christian.

27. Muslims constitute 2 per cent of France's population according to the *World Guide 1999/2000*, p.256.

28. See Jean Lacouture, 1974. *Nasser.* New York: Alfred Knopf, p.388, and for an extended discussion of Nasser's ideology, consult Nissim Rejwan, 1974: *Nasserist Ideology: Its Exponents and Critics.* New York and Toronto; Jerusalem: John Wiley and Sons; Israel Universities.

29. Nkrumah, 1957. *Ghana: The Autobiography of Kwame Nkrumah.* London and New York: T. H. Nelson and seventh edition, International Publishers, 1989, p.12.

30. The marriage is described in Rooney, Kwame Nkrumah: *The Political Kingdom in the Third World*, pp. 144–145.

31. Rooney, p.251.

32. See, for example, William B. Ackah, 1999: *Pan-Africanism: Exploring the Contradiction: Politics, Identity And Development in Africa and the African Diaspora.* Aldershot, Hants, England, Broofield, Vt., USA: Ashgate.

33. Mazrui, A., 1966: "Kwame Nkrumah: The Leninist Czar," *Transition*, pp. 9–17.

LECTURE 2

NKRUMAHISM IN THE SHADOW OF COUNTER-
TERRORISM

In the last lecture, we explored globalization as the product of four engines of change: religion, technology, economy and empire. We postulated that globalization could be either positive or negative, depending upon the values it realized.[1] We also introduced Kwame Nkrumah's concept of **consciencism** as a convergence of three civilizations: Africanity, Islam and Western culture.[2] I renamed this convergence and called it **Africa's triple heritage**.[3]

In this second lecture, we take the concept of globalization beyond Africa itself. Is there such a thing as **Global Africa**? Has the Black experience itself been globalized — with Ghana as a major actor in that globalization? And how does all this relate to the shadows of terrorism and counter-terrorism in the new age?

Two African countries in the 1950s were symbolic of alternative ways of confronting imperialism. One of those countries was Kenya, which entered the era of the Mau Mau struggle, a struggle which was roundly denounced in much of the Western world as **terrorism**. The Mau Mau fighters in Kenya often tried to kill civilians in colonial Kenya — ranging from white farming families to Black African apologists for British rule. It was demonstrable that Mau Mau was to some extent a terrorist movement.[4]

The other African country in the 1950s constantly in the news was the Gold Coast. What was distinctive about the Gold Coast's struggle for independence was that it was not violent, and was far removed from terrorism.[5] On the contrary, Kwame Nkrumah sometimes claimed to be a disciple of Mahatma Gandhi. Nkrumah's Positive Action as a strategy was partly defined in non-violent Gandhian terms.

The British Empire in Africa was, therefore, faced with two alternative models of decolonization. In Kenya, it was a racial confrontation between Black nationalists on one side and stubborn and deeply-entrenched white settlers on the other. The Kenyan model of decolonization was steeped in violence and terrorism on both sides — both state terrorism and violence by Mau Mau.

In the Gold Coast, on the other hand, the model of decolonization was one of peaceful constitutional change. Under the Convention People's Party and Kwame Nkrumah, there was indeed political agitation and strong pressure on the colonial order.[6] However, there was no organized political violence or guerilla movement for the independence of the Gold Coast.

The violent Mau Mau struggle in Kenya and the Gandhian-like struggle in the Gold Coast were truly antithetical as decolonizing strategies. But then, independence came to Ghana in 1957. In the following year (December 1958), Ghana hosted the All Africa People's Conference in Accra. On the one hand, the conference elected Kenya's Tom Mboya to preside.[7] That appeared to be a partial recognition to the nationalist movement in Kenya in spite of the fact that Tom Mboya was not personally involved with Mau Mau.

This December 1958 conference was the successor conference to the First Conference of Independent African States (CIAS), held earlier that year also in Accra. At the CIAS, states were still inclined toward a policy of peaceful action toward decolonization. Its declarations on the Algerian struggle for independence from France were largely condemnatory of the colonial policies, but appealed for an end to violence and for a negotiated settlement.[8]

But in time, Africa came to accept armed struggle as a legitimate strategy of decolonization either in those societies with entrenched white settler power (such as Rhodesia or South Africa) or in those African countries which were regarded by the imperial power as provinces of the metropole and, therefore, never to be eligible for independence (such as the Portuguese colonies). In such societies, terrorism as a form of violent intimidation was perpetrated by both sides.

Kwame Nkrumah became a major defender of the rights of liberation movements in Southern Africa. Whether liberation movements in Angola, Mozambique or Rhodesia were adequately armed or not became a major Nkrumahist concern both when he was in power and afterwards. Terrorism became an acceptable strategy of decolonization. After all, where does terrorism begin?

After September 11, 2001, however, had Africa itself been redefined? Is there a new concept called "Global Africa"? Has there been a redefinition of where a war of liberation ends and a war against terrorism begins?

After September 11, has the South lost its right to define its own scale of priorities? Let us look more closely at some of the basics of this unfolding equation.

2.1   Between King and Malcolm X

There is indeed a concept called "Global Africa." It means the people of Africa and those of African descent who are scattered all over the world. The late C.L.R. James of Trinidad talked about "What do they know of cricket who only cricket know."[9] But, in fact, much more relevant is to paraphrase the original British poem (Rudyard Kipling's "The English Flag") in the following way:

> Winds of the world give answer
> They are whimpering to and fro
> Who should know of Africa
> Who only Africa know.

Although, as president of Ghana, Kwame Nkrumah paid special emphasis to the unification of African **continent**, his ultimate vision was that of "**Global Africa**." He regarded himself as in part a Garveyite Black nationalist, committed to the links between Africa and its Diaspora.

Nkrumah welcomed the participation of Diaspora Blacks in building Ghana.[10] George Padmore of the Caribbean and W. E. B. Du Bois of the United States became citizens of Ghana, died in Ghana and are buried there.[11]

Anti-colonial movements in Africa coincided with civil rights movement in the United States. The two sets of movements reinforced each other.[12] Dr. Martin Luther King Jr. monitored anti-colonialism and mobilized the civil rights movement. They constituted the liberal face of globalization.

Somewhere between them stood Malcolm X (el-Hajj Malik El Shabazz) — closer to Muslim mujahidden in radicalism and militancy, yet closer to Martin Luther King in the experience of white racism.[13] These two Diaspora Africans touched my life **very briefly**, and each symbolized something important to Global Africa. Each of these Diaspora Africans was assassinated. Such assassinations were cases of individualized terrorism.

I met Martin Luther King Jr. in New York within months of my meeting Kwame Nkrumah. I was a graduate student at Columbia

University. I was impressed that King knew so much about Kenya and knew the African politician Tom Mboya personally, who was then a rising political star of Kenya. Of course, King and Nkrumah also knew each other personally.

Partly because he was a Reverend, and partly because of his Biblical oratory, I might have regarded Martin Luther King as a link between Global Africa and Christendom, though I could not have articulated it in quite that fashion at that age.

The second Diaspora martyr who touched my life very briefly was Malcolm X. I also met him in New York in the early 1960s. Since I had myself been brought up a Muslim, I was fascinated by Malcolm's creed. I disagreed with his racial approach to Islam at that stage of his life, but I was thrilled by his political militancy. He also had a magnetic personal presence. In terms of Global Africa, was he one of its important links with the global *ummah*?

If Martin Luther King was a link between Global Africa and Christianity and Malcolm X a link between Global Africa and Islam, Kwame Nkrumah was in part a link between Global Africa and the world of Socialism. The political careers of King, Malcolm and Nkrumah all ended abruptly in the 1960s. King and Malcolm were assassinated. Nkrumah was overthrown in a military coup.

Since Martin Luther King was a link between Global Africa and Christianity, his memory found it easier to acquire legitimacy in the Western world. Martin King's birthday has even acquired greater official status than Abraham Lincoln's birthday. Although harassed by the Federal Bureau of Investigation (FBI) when he was alive, and constantly under the shadow of right-wing extremists in the United States, Reverend King was, in the ultimate analysis, a preferred antagonist of the Establishment.[14] Kwame Nkrumah lost the admiration of the Western establishment half way through his presidential career.

Yet, at first, King and Nkrumah were both disciples of Mahatma Gandhi — a far cry from terrorism. Nkrumah's strategy of "Positive Action" was intended to be as non-violent as Gandhi's soul force. Ghana's struggle for independence was partly Gandhian.

However, partly because Malcolm X was a link between Blackness and Islam, he has yet to be restored to national legitimacy in the United States. No scholarships nor major schools have been named after him. How is the legacy of Malcolm related to the horrific events of September 11?

Malcolm X's **bark** was more ferocious than his bite. Philosophically, he believed that people should fight for their **legitimate** rights "**by any means necessary**" (Malcolm's words).[15] Philosophically, Malcolm was prepared to accept violence and perhaps even terrorism, provided the cause was morally right. After all, the American Revolution itself was a revolution of violence and war.

Malcolm was Muslim by religious affiliation and an African by descent. Was it his Muslim side which embraced the doctrine "by any means necessary"? Did Malcolm envisage a kind of **racial** *jihad*?[16]

Or were both his Black nationalism and his religious fervor radical enough to embrace the principle of "by any means necessary"? Malcolm X was perhaps the nearest equivalent to Nkrumah that Black America has produced. Malcolm was a Triple Heritage radical —combining Pan-African nationalism, strong Islamic empathy and the reality of Western roots.[17]

2.2 Ku Klux Klan as a Terrorist Movement

When Nkrumah was a student in America, racism was still institutionalized in the South. The Ku Klux Klan (KKK) was one of the best illustrations of racism — motivated by terrorism.

The history of terror in the American experience is a transition from individualized terrorism from within the United States to collective terrorism from outside the United States. Individualized terrorism is the tormenting or killing of individual civilians by other civilians for racial, ideological, or other political reasons. Under this definition Ku Klux Klan (KKK) was a terrorist organization — designed to create terror and consternation among particular vulnerable groups in the society.

The Ku Klux Klan was the most durable and longest surviving terrorist organization in the history of the United States. More than a century before Al-Qaeda, there was Al-Klan. More than a century before Usama bin Laden there was the Grand Wizard Nathan Forrest. In 1867, the Klan was declared "the Invisible Empire of the South" at a convention in Nashville. Nathan Bedford Forrest was the first Grand Wizard. In the nineteenth century, the KKK started as a social club by Confederate veterans in Pulaski, Tennessee in 1866. The name was apparently derived from the Greek *Kuklos*, meaning approximately "circle". Indeed, the English word "circle" is derived from it. The "suffix" *Klan* was added for alliterative reasons.[18]

KKK became a vehicle for Southern White underground resistance to Radical Reconstruction. The KKK struggled to restore White supremacy in the South by whipping and killing freed Blacks and their White supporters. They wore white robes and sheets to maximize the terror to their Black victims.

In night raids, they did not cry out "Allah Akbar" (God is great), but they often used the burning cross for further intimidation. White supremacy in Tennessee, North Carolina and Georgia was indeed restored partly as a result of Klan action.

In response to continuing violence among local KKK branches, the US Congress started legislating in ways which threatened the civil liberties of White folk. Congress passed the Force Act of 1870 and Ku Klux Klan Act of 1871 authorizing the President to suspend the writ of habeas corpus, suppress KKK disturbances by force, and impose heavy fines on such terrorist organizations.[19]

President Ulysses S.Grant sent federal troops to some areas, suspended habeas corpus for some counties in South Carolina, and detained hundreds of Southerners for conspiracy.[20] Such strong measures against White people was something new.

Positive Nkrumahism are those aspects of his legacy which are constructive and good for the future. **Negative Nkrumahism** are those aspects which are related to his legacy of authoritarianism.

When the United States joined up with Canada and Mexico to form NAFTA (North American Free Trade Agreement), that was a kind of positive Nkrumahism of Pan-Americanism. But, since September 11, the United States has shown symptoms of negative Nkrumahism.

In the 19th century, civil liberties in the United States were curtailed by an act of Congress. Since September 11, 2001, civil liberties are curtailed at the initiative of Attorney General John Ashcroft. When Nkrumah was in power, it is unlikely that he learnt about curtailing civil liberties from the Americans. But, since September 11, one sometimes wonders whether the US learnt some bad lessons from Nkrumah. In America since September 11:

1. There are hundreds of people in detention without trial.[21]

2. The great majority of those in detention are not publicly announced as being in detention.[22] Nkrumah detained without trial, but the prisoners were publicly known as a rule.

3. Out of the hundreds in detention, in 2002 in the United States, less than a **dozen** show any evidence of knowing any particular terrorist suspect or being associated with any movement or charity accused of terrorism. Such indifference to evidence of guilt was also part of negative Nkrumahism.

4. Out of the millions of illegal immigrants in the United States, and those whose visas have expired, the people chosen by the Bush administration for detention without trial are almost certainly those with Muslim names or who come from the Middle East or South Asia.[23] Nkrumah's regime was sometimes also guilty of ethnic profiling, but perhaps never as blatantly.

5. The United States is actually planning to have military tribunals and secret trials for those suspected of terrorism.[24] Even the leaders of Nazi Germany were given a public trial at Nuremberg after World War II with access to counsel and proper representation. Some of those tried at Nuremberg had been responsible for the death of millions of people.[25] Negative Nkrumahism sometimes also showed inadequate respect for open trials, but negative military ones are more Ashcroftian than Nkrumahist.

6. Some of the strategies contemplated by the USA and by Israel are much worse than anything done by Kwame Nkrumah's regime even at its worst. Israel continues to look for old **Nazi** militants so that they can be **tried** today in a **court of law** in Israel. Yet, Israel feels free to kill Palestinian militants instead of capturing them for trial. Israel tried Adolf Eichmann in 1961 and protected him at the trial with a bulletproof glass cage so that he would not be assassinated.[26] Yet, both the USA and Israel in 2001 openly talked about killing terrorist suspects instead of capturing them. And even when Israel has illegally captured Palestinian or Lebanese suspects from across its own borders, the purpose has almost never been to give them a fair trial (Adolf Eichmann-style) but to detain those suspects indefinitely **without trial**. When Nkrumah denounced Israel in 1961 as a tool of global imperialism, was Nkrumah ahead of his time?[27]

7. US Attorney General John Ashcroft has empowered the FBI to

spy on churches, mosques, synagogues and other sacred places to an extent not envisaged in the country for a long time. Places of prayer were once protected from close police scrutiny. However, mosques especially may soon be fair game for police raids in American cities. Will **synagogues** enjoy *de facto* protection even if there is militant Zionism or fundamentalist Judaism being preached inside? The Nkrumah regime has a better record of equal protection for religious institutions.

8. US Attorney-General Ashcroft wants to breach attorney-client confidentiality if the client is suspected of terrorism.[28] The Attorney General and President Bush repeatedly talk as if those **suspected** of terrorism were already **proven** terrorists. What happened to the US principle that a person was innocent until proven guilty? On this issue, the United States is moving dangerously close once again to Nkrumah's relative lack of respect for the judiciary, an aspect of negative Nkrumahism.

9. CNN and the other major TV networks in the United States were summoned to the White House and warned against giving Osama bin Laden propaganda advantage with his videos. What happened to editorial independence and freedom of the Press? Is this the slippery slope towards Press censorship in Nkrumah style of Negative Nkrumahism?

10. President Bush described the attacks of September 11 as "an act of war" and responded with war in Afghanistan. Yet prisoners of Al-Qaeda and Taliban fighters are denied the rights of prisoners of war according to the Geneva convention.[29] Even US allies in Europe are disturbed that the US is slipping away from civilized standards and from obeying international laws. Nkrumah had political prisoners rather than prisoners of war.

Let us return to the earlier years of racial terrorism in the United States. In the 20th century, the new Ku Klux Klan rose near Atlanta, Georgia, in 1915. At its peak, this terrorist organization in the United States had four million members nation-wide. Its agenda of prejudice had widened. In addition to being anti-Black, it became anti-Catholic, especially in 1928 when Alfred E. Smith, a Catholic, won the nomination of the Democratic Party for President. The new KKK was also anti-Jewish, anti-immigrant, and against organized labour.[30]

One of the most pernicious kinds of violence against the other was lynching.[31] The victims of the KKK's lynching were overwhelmingly Black. Nkrumah was partly educated in a Black college, Lincoln University. But Pennsylvania was in the less racist North. Lynchings in the South continued into the second half of the 20th century, though their numbers had drastically declined. Some of the lynchings were perpetrated by supporters of KKK who were not necessarily members. NAACP organizers were killed in Mississippi while trying to register Black voters in the 1950s. These included **Reverend George W. Lee** and **Lamar Smith**.[32]

The most shocking lynching of the 1950s was the 1955 murder of a fourteen–year old Black boy Emmett Till, who was visiting Mississippi from Chicago, and was dared by other Black boys to say something courageous to a White woman in a shop. Emmett Till gathered enough courage to say to the White woman "Bye, Baby"! As a Northern boy from Chicago, he was showing off he could do something daring to a White woman.

Those two words not only cost the boy's life. He was picked up, tortured, had an eye pulled out, shot in the head, chained to a seventy-five pound cotton gin and thrown into a river to sink. The body surfaced a few days later and was identified. An all-White jury returned a verdict of "**Not guilty**" on people who had kidnapped Emmett Till and must have been the ones who killed him. They were even acquitted of kidnapping. But for the first time in the history of Mississippi, a Black man testified against an accused White man. Mose Wright, Emmett's uncle, found the courage to identify the White folks who had picked up his nephew. Courage is different from fearlessness. Courage is to be afraid and still be able to do what needs to be done. Mose Wright was courageous in that court as he pointed out the kidnappers of his nephew.[33]

It took the murder of a White woman ten years later in Alabama before the President of the United States would go on television to publicly denounce the Ku Klux Klan. President Lyndon Johnson at last condemned the organization in March 1965 in a nationwide television broadcast. He also announced the arrest of four Klansmen for the murder of the civil rights worker — a White woman in Alabama.[34]

Yet even in the 1990s it was still possible for a Black man to be tied at the back of White man's truck and dragged until his head rolled off his body. Individualized racial terrorism was still alive and well in the United States when in 1998 James Byrd Jr. was chained behind a pick-up truck in Jasper, Texas, and mutilated in this manner by a couple of White racists.[35] Racially-inspired terrorism in the United States existed long before Nkrumah went to America — and long after he left.

Nevertheless, September 11, 2001 took terrorism to entirely new levels of destructiveness. It was not the terrorism of the powerful against the vulnerable, as in the case of the KKK violence against underprivileged Blacks. September 11, 2001 was terrorism against the most powerful in the world. The Pentagon was a symbol of America's military might. The World Trade Centre was a symbol of America's economic might. If Al-Qaeda were the terrorists of September 11, 2001, this was action by cave-dwellers against the super-rich and the super-powerful. It was criminal and cruel, but it was David fighting Goliath, and in this case David came to pay a heavy price. While the KKK picked on vulnerable minorities to terrorize, Al-Qaeda has picked on the mightiest power to challenge. The result has been catastrophic for both sides.

If movements of Arab or Afghan cave-dwellers are a case of "Muslim David", what are the causes of the rage against the American Goliath? It may be best to use as a comparison another previously-colonized region — Africa. Let us engage in a study of comparative violence between weak societies and strong external powers.

2.3 Colonized David and Imperial Goliath

Why has terrorism continued to escalate in the Middle East while it has declined in Africa? Why is Africa talking about "Truth and Reconciliation" and Reparations from the White man — while the Arabs are still proclaiming **Jihad**?

Why do Arab militants regard "Pay Back Time" in terms of retribution against the West — while so many African nationalists regard "Pay Back Time" in terms of reparation from the West? Do Muslim militants share Malcolm X's insistence that legitimate rights should be fought for "by any means necessary"?

Let us now look much more closely at the dynamics of politics in Africa and the Middle East from the point of view of reparation *versus* retribution between colonized David and imperial Goliath.

The 2001 conference in Durban, South Africa, against racism and xenophobia took the issues of reparations forward.[36] But the terrorist events in New York on September 11, 2001 might have caused a setback to the cause of reparations. Both Durban and September 11 have demonstrated once again a link between Africa and the Middle East, and the link has been affected by the forces of globalization.

Kwame Nkrumah did not really address the issue of restitution. I would like to explore the issue of reparations, on one side, and terrorist retribution, on the other, as alternative methods of "PAY BACK." I would like to place Africa alongside the Middle East in comparative perspective. Africa and the Middle East are in any case overlapping regions.

Imperialism in the Middle East provoked the worst levels of anti-Western terrorism **after** formal liberation from European colonial rule. The British had been in power in Egypt, Iraq, Jordan, Sudan and elsewhere. The French had been in power in Syria, Lebanon, Algeria, Morocco, Tunisia and elsewhere. Palestine had been a United Nations trusteeship under British administration.

Imperialism in Africa provoked the worst levels of anti-Western terrorism **before** formal liberation from European colonial rule: that is to say, before Independence Day. We began by discussing the Mau Mau revolt in colonial Kenya. Let us also relate the comparison to comparative rage. Imperialism in Africa triggered the most explosive anti-Western anger **before** European colonialists left Africa. Imperialism in the Middle East triggered off the most explosive anti-Western anger **after** European colonialists had left the Arab world.

What the colonial powers and white minority governments had condemned as "terrorism" in Africa included the Mau Mau war in Kenya, and the liberation wars in Algeria, Angola, Zimbabwe, Guinea (Bissau), Mozambique, and South Africa. In and out of office, Nkrumah supported Liberation wars. What the Western world has condemned as "terrorism" in the Middle East has included hostage taking in Lebanon, hijacking of planes in the 1970s, as well as suicide bombs in the streets of Israel. The most spectacular was the destruction of the World Trade Centre and the attack on the Pentagon on September 11, 2001.

In what sense are we to conclude that while the impact of imperialism in the Middle East created conditions for **violent** "PAY BACK" against the West, the impact of imperialism on Africa has been to create conditions which are ideal for "PAY BACK" in terms of **reparations** from the West?

Some of the differences between Africa and the Middle East are **situational**, while other differences are primarily **cultural**. The postcolonial situation in the Middle East included a **permanent loss** of territory imposed by outsiders. The postcolonial situation in Africa involved **recovery** of territory — including recovery of land previously parceled out by apartheid in South Africa. This was won back to Africa.

Africa had also been spared the forceful creation of a **Jewish state in Uganda** and Kenya earlier in the 20th century. **Joseph Chamberlain**, the British Colonial Secretary at the time, had offered **Theodor Herzl**, the leader of the Zionist movement, a piece of Uganda and a piece of Kenya at the beginning of the 20th century for the creation of a new Jewish state. (The boundaries of Uganda early in the 20th century included parts of present-day Kenya).

Had the Zionist movement accepted the offer, and a permanent Jewish state been established in East Africa, it is conceivable that African anger against the West today would be comparable to anti-Western rage in the Middle East.

But the Zionist movement in 1903 could not reach consensus about creating "Israel" in East Africa — and therefore the postcolonial situation in Africa today involves no permanent loss of territory.[37]

A related situational difference is that while the postcolonial conditions in Africa meant a clear end of foreign occupation, the postcolonial situation in the Middle East carried new forms of foreign occupation. It involved **not** just the creation of the state of Israel but also the occupation by Israel of the West Bank of the Jordan, the occupation of Gaza, the annexation of the Golan Heights of Syria, the annexation of the whole of Jerusalem and the occupation for a while of a piece of Southern Lebanon. While the postcolonial period in Africa is truly post-occupation, the postcolonial period in the Middle East has entailed new forms of territorial annexations.

Where does the United States fit into this equation? When European powers occupied Africa and parts of Asia, **the image of America was that of an anti-colonial force** in world affairs. The United States put a lot of pressure on its European allies to speed up the process of giving independence to the colonies.

Even as late as 1956 — when Britain, France and Israel invaded Egypt in response to Egypt's nationalization of the Suez Canal — the Eisenhower Administration turned against its allies. The United States forced Israel to withdraw from the Sinai, and forced Britain and France to give up Port Said in Egypt. The British Prime Minister had a nervous breakdown — Anthony Eden gave way to Harold McMillan.

Egypt's Nasser emerged as a world figure — partly because the United States would not support the Anglo-Franco-Israeli invasion of Egypt. Nasser had been militarily defeated, but emerged politically triumphant. The Eisenhower administration — wittingly or unwittingly — had helped the Egyptian president rise to global stature.[38]

John F. Kennedy as President dismissed the concerns of the white settlers elsewhere in Africa when they objected to the phrase "AFRICA FOR THE AFRICANS." When Kennedy, at a news conference, was asked by reporters if he agreed with the phrase, first uttered by his Assistant Secretary of State, "Soapy" Williams at a press conference in Nairobi, Kennedy retorted, "I don't know who else Africa would be for."[39] The United State was on the side of the aspirations of African nationalists.

But two things were happening which future historians would later have to disentangle. The United States was expanding towards greater globalization and increasing its role of interventionism in other parts of the world. In the second half of the 20th century, the United States began to be seen more and more as an imperial power, and a supporter of Israel policies of occupation and repression.

WHY IS THE U.S. being blamed for Israel policies? Where is Usama bin Laden's anti-Americanism coming from? The following are some of the salient factors.

1. Massive economic aid from the United States to Israel in billions.[40]
2. Provision of sophisticated American weapons to Israel.
3. The United States shielding Israel from U.N. censure.
4. The United States making U.N. Security Council impotent in punishing Israel.
5. The United States policy of weakening anti-Israeli Arab forces by buying off the government of Egypt with a billion U.S. dollars every year. Egypt is the largest Arab country in population and used to be the biggest single threat to Israel militarily. The U.S. largess has bought off Egypt effectively.[41]

6. Preventing **Iraq** from rising as an alternative to Egypt in challenging Israel.

7. Taking advantage of Iraq's invasion of Kuwait to weaken Iraq permanently. Pearl Harbor was not used to weaken Japan permanently, nor was Hitler's aggression used to weaken Germany permanently.

The **United States** is the main source of military support for the enemy of the Arab World, Israel, and the USA is also the main destroyer of Arab capacity to rise militarily. This latter policy includes weakening Egypt and enfeebling Iraq.

The American base in Saudi Arabia since 1991 is perceived as turning sacred Islamic soil into an extension of the Pentagon. The American base in Saudi Arabia is seen not as a shield against such external enemies as Saddam Hussein, but a shield against an internal Iran-style Islamic revolution in Saudi Arabia. A situation of gross military frustration has been created, especially in Palestine and Iraq, but also on the sacred sands of Saudi Arabia.[42]

2.4 Comparative Rage and Cultural Differences

But the differences between Africa and the Middle East in relation to political **rage** are not only due to divergent post-colonial situations. There are also basic differences in **culture** between the Arabo-Hebrew Semitic peoples (both Arabs and Jews) on one side, and the majority of Black people in sub-Saharan Africa.

One major difference is the martyrdom complex which is much more developed among Middle Eastern peoples than among the Bantu and other peoples of sub-Saharan Africa. The link between heroism and suicide among the Jews goes back to **Masada**, the site of the Jews' final resistance against the Romans after the fall of the Temple in year 70 C.E. The brave defenders finally committed suicide rather than surrender.

The Jews have more recently fashioned memories of the Holocaust into a major doctrine of Jewish martyrdom in history.[43] As for readiness to commit collective suicide, the Israeli nuclear program is partly based on the premise of the Samson option — a readiness to defend Israel even if it means destroying it and much of the rest of the region.

Among Muslims of the Middle East (both Arab and Iranian), there is also the martyrdom complex in varying degrees.[44] Historically, it has been more developed among Shi'a Muslims than among Sunni.[45] Suicide bombers against Israel and American troops in Lebanon started among Shiite Lebanese. The martyrdom complex among the Shi'a goes back to the suffering and martyrdom of Imam Hussein, the grandson of the Prophet Mohammad.

But anger against Israel and the United States has now resulted in the extension of the martyrdom complex to the Sunni population of the Middle East.

Because culturally the Middle East has a martyrdom complex which is much more highly developed than among any groups in sub-Saharan Africa, it is the Middle East which has been readier than Africa to commit suicidal political violence against the West. In the postcolonial period, it is the Middle East, more than Africa, which has been ready to engage in acts of suicidal terrorism against the West.

Another major cultural difference between the Middle East and Africa concerns **comparative hate retention**. Cultures differ in hate-retention. Some cultures preserve a grudge across centuries. The Irish of Northern Ireland quarrel every year about a Protestant victory of the Orange order against Catholics four centuries ago. The Irish have a high hate-retentive capacity.

The Armenian massacres of 1915 by the Ottoman Empire are still remembered bitterly by Armenians — and from time to time, this memory results in the assassination of a Turkish diplomat somewhere in the world.[46]

The Jews also have high hate-retentiveness, but they have sublimated it through the martyrdom complex. The Holocaust is given a sacred meaning rather than merely remembered as hate. There are many Jews in the world who feel that Germany must remain an external enemy. Such Jews would not buy German products, watch German movies, travel to Germany or listen to the music of Richard Wagner.

Because the Arabs have had a vastly different history from Jews in the last fourteen centuries, the Arabs' experience as a persecuted people is relatively recent. Their hate-retention and their martyrdom complex is not as well developed or as sophisticated as that of the Jews. But Arabs and Jews do both share a fascination with the martyrdom complex.

Now contrast this culturally with Black Africa. A major reason why Black Africa has not produced postcolonial political violence against the West is Africa's short memory of hate. **Mahatma Gandhi** used to prophesize that it would probably be through Black people that the unadulterated message of soul force [*satyagraha*] and passive resistance might be realized.[47] Younger Nkrumah was a disciple of Gandhi; but was Gandhi correct in this estimate? If Gandhi was indeed right, this could be one more illustration of comparative hate-retention.

The Nobel Committee for Peace in Oslo seems to have shared some of Gandhi's optimism about the soul force of the Black people. Africans and people of African descent who have won the Nobel Prize for Peace since the middle of the 20th century have been Ralph Bunche (1950), Albert Luthuli (1960), Martin Luther King Jr. (1964), Anwar Sadat (1978), Desmond Tutu (1984) and Nelson Mandela (1993). And now (2001), Kofi Annan and his U.N. leadership have joined the galaxy. Neither Mahatma Gandhi himself nor any of his compatriots in India ever won the Nobel Prize for Peace, though Indians have won other categories of the Nobel Prize. Was Mahatma Gandhi vindicated that the so-called "Negro" was going to be the best exemplar of soul force? Was this a case of African culture being empirically more Gandhi than Indian culture?

In reality, Black people have been at least as violent as anything ever perpetrated by Indians. The Horn of Africa has had its fair share of violence. So have other parts of Black Africa. What is distinctive about Africans is their short memory of hate. Jomo Kenyatta was unjustly imprisoned by the British colonial authorities over charges of founding the Mau Mau "terrorist" movement. A British Governor also denounced him as "a leader unto darkness and unto death." And yet when Jomo Kenyatta was released he not only forgave the White settlers, but turned the whole country towards a basic pro-Western orientation to which it has remained committed ever since. Kenyatta even published a book entitled *Suffering Without Bitterness*.[48]

During Nkrumah's last years in office, Ian Smith, the White settler leader of Rhodesia, unilaterally declared independence. This unleashed a civil war on Rhodesia. Thousands of people, mainly Black, died in the country as a result of policies pursued by Ian Smith from 1965 onwards. Yet, when the war ended in 1980 Ian Smith and his cohorts were **not** subjected to a Nuremberg-style trial. On the contrary, Ian Smith was himself elected as a member of parliament in a Black-ruled Zimbabwe, and was busy criticizing the post-Smith Black leaders of Zimbabwe as incompetent and dishonest.[49] Where else but in Africa could such tolerance occur?

The Nigerian civil war (1967–1970) was the most highly publicized civil conflict in postcolonial African history. When the war was coming to an end, many people feared that there would be a bloodbath in the defeated eastern region. The Vatican was worried that cities like Enugu and Onitcha, strongholds of Catholicism, would be monuments of devastation and bloodletting.[50]

None of these expectations occurred. Nigerians — seldom among the most disciplined of Africans — discovered in 1970 some remarkable resources of self-restraint. There were no triumphant or triumphalist reprisals against the vanquished Biafrans; there were no vengeful trials of "traitors".

We have also witnessed the phenomenon of Nelson Mandela.[51] He lost twenty-seven of the best years of his life in prison under the laws of the apartheid regime. Yet, when he was released, he not only emphasized the policy of reconciliation — he often went beyond the call of duty. On one occasion before he became President, White men were fasting unto death after being convicted of terrorist offenses by their own White government. Nelson Mandela went out of his way to beg them to eat and thus spare their own lives.

When Mandela became President in 1994, it was surely enough that his government would leave the architects of apartheid unmolested. Yet, Nelson Mandela went out of his way to pay a social call and have tea with the unrepentant widow of Hendrik F. Verwoed, the supreme architect of the worst forms of apartheid, who shaped the whole racist order from 1958 to 1966. Mandela was having tea with the family of Verwoed.[52]

Was Mahatma Gandhi correct, after all, that his torch of soul force (*satyagraha*) might find its brightest manifestations among Black people? Empirical relativism was at work again.

In the history of civilizations, there are occasions when the image in the mirror is more real than the object it reflects. Black Gandhians like Martin Luther King Jr., Desmond Tutu and, in a unique sense, Nelson Mandela have sometimes reflected Gandhaian soul force more brightly than Gandhians in India. Part of the explanation lies in the soul of African culture itself — with all its capacity for rapid forgiveness.[53]

Africans can be brutal to each other. Some commit **genocide** — as the Hutu did to the Tutsi in Rwanda in 1994. Other Africans commit **regicide** — murdering their Kings or their Presidents and former Presidents. But when all is said and done, is there room for Truth and Reconciliation in Africa?

Yet, "PAY BACK" as an African demand, is a claim for reparations — contrasting sharply with "PAY BACK" as political retribution against the West, by other damaged regions of the world. The West should respond positively to this softer, gentler version of "PAY BACK TIME" between the West and the Rest. Better the music of reparations than the drums of terror.

2.5 Harbouring Terrorists *versus* Protecting Freedom Fighters?

In the year 2001, President George Bush declared war not just on terrorists but also on those who harbour terrorists.

In the days of Nkrumah, harboring terrorists in Africa was often harboring liberation fighters. To Nkrumah, any country that offers sanctuary to freedom fighters must earn that honor. Harboring freedom fighters was not a vice (like George Bush wants it to be), but a privilege in the eyes of Nkrumah.

Tanzania was a haven for liberation fighters of Southern Africa. Nyerere was sensitive to the danger of having his credentials questioned or compromised as a result of Nkrumah's initiative. And so, when in January 1964 Nyerere was compelled by circumstances to invite British troops to re-enter his country in order to disarm his own local military mutineers, the Mwalimu was so conscious of his vulnerability to critics like Nkrumah that he immediately invited the Organization of African Unity (OAU) to meet in Dar es Salaam and hear an explanation of why he had been forced to invite British troops. So keen was he to protect his country from the stigma of neo-dependency that he was prepared to risk incurring the displeasure of Kenya and Uganda rather than compromise his Pan-African respectability. His independent initiative to invite the OAU to Dar es Salaam did in fact irritate the two other East African countries that had been similarly forced to invite British troops to disarm their own mutinous soldiers. Obote of Uganda was impelled to express public skepticism about the utility of the cleansing ceremony in Dar es Salaam.

Was the ceremony effective in cleansing Nyerere's reputation? By the time the heads of African states met in Cairo in the middle of 1964, Nkrumah was prepared to state his skeptical position officially. He doubted the credentials of Dar es Salaam as the headquarters of liberation movements in the light of Dar es Salaam's readiness to invite British troops in. Admittedly, by that time, Nyerere had taken the precaution of asking the British troops to leave and having them replaced by Nigerian troops in Tanganyika. But from Nkrumah's point of view, the harm had been done. A country that could actually take the initiative to invite troops of her former colonial ruler, and then express public gratitude to her former colonial ruler for that loan of troops, could not be trusted as the headquarters of African liberation movements. Nkrumah was, therefore, asking the OAU to reconsider the decision to entrust liberation to a capital like Dar es Salaam.

Nyerere was indignant. He went public with his attack on Nkrumah. He referred to people who pretended that they were in favor of African continental union when all they cared about was to ensure that "some stupid historian in the future" praised them for being in favor of the big continental ambition before anyone else was willing to undertake it. Nyerere added snide remarks about "the Redeemer" (Nkrumah's self-embraced title of the *Osagyefo*). On balance, history has proved Nkrumah wrong on the question of Nyerere's commitment to liberation. Nyerere was second to none in that commitment.

At that Cairo conference of 1964, Nkrumah had said "what could be the result of entrusting the training of Freedom Fighters against imperialism into the hands of an imperialist agent? Nyerere had indeed answered "the good Osagyefo" with sarcasm and counter-argument. But Nyerere was also already trying to sharpen his country's militancy in anti-colonial policy. At Cairo, he took the posture of a leader disillusioned with the arts of persuasion in matters of liberation. He now demanded rigorous action to expel Portugal from Africa. As he put it:

> I am convinced that the finer the words the greater the harm they do to the prestige of Africa if they are not followed by action . . . Africa is strong enough to drive Portugal from our Continent. Let us resolve at this conference to take the necessary action.[54]

Nyerere did indeed attempt to take the lead in this new militancy. He became the toughest spokesman against the British on the Rhodesian question. His country played a crucial role at the OAU Ministerial meeting at which it was decided to issue that fatal ultimatum to Britain's Prime Minister, Harold Wilson– "Break Ian Smith or Africa will break with you." After Nkrumah was overthrown in February 1966, Julius Nyerere became the leading radical voice of Africa in support of armed liberation. Was Nyerere partly radicalized by the taunts of Kwame Nkrumah?[55]

We have emphasized Nkrumah's belief that Africa was molded by three civilizations — African, Islamic and Western. But in this lecture we have witnessed the globalization of terrorism and the globalization of Africa itself.

2.6 Towards Globalizing King's Dream

Martin Luther King Jr. was politically molded by two personal forces external to the Black experience. In the case of King, the two external personalities were Jesus Christ and Mahatma Gandhi.

Many people believe that Lenin operationalized Marx from the world of ideas to the world of policy. King believed that Gandhi operationalized the love-ethic of Jesus from the world of ethics to the world of action.

Both of Martin Luther King's ultimate mentors were, in a sense, assassinated. The Jesus of Christianity was assassinated through the crucifixion. Mahatma Gandhi was assassinated by a bullet from a fellow Hindu. The crucifixion of Jesus was an act of state terrorism. The assassination of Gandhi was privatized terrorism. Nkrumah, too, acknowledged a debt to both Gandhi and to non-denominational Christianity.

King used the legacy of soul-force from Jesus and Gandhi as a means to an end. The end was the liberation and dignification of Black people. For Martin Luther King Jr., the union between Jesus Christ and Mohandas Gandhi was indissoluble. If Christianity had been, like Hinduism, a religion based on **reincarnation**, Reverend King would have wondered whether Mohandas Gandhi was a reincarnation of Jesus Christ. At least so far the union between Jesus and Gandhi has turned out to be more truly indissoluble than the union between Marx and Lenin. Nkrumah was nevertheless fascinated by Marx and Lenin more enduringly than by Jesus and Gandhi.

Martin Luther King's dream remains relevant, but it needs to be globalized. It needs to reconcile not just different races, but different civilizations. This is particularly urgent since September 11, 2001. Nkrumah was global almost from the start. King needs internationalization. Nkrumah's *I Speak of Freedom* and *Stride Towards Freedom* show abiding preoccupation with liberty.

So, let freedom ring from the shores of Somalia and the high plateaus of Ethiopia; let freedom ring from the deep valley of the Brahmaputra and Euphrates; let freedom ring from the isles of the Caribbean and the deep recesses of the Amazon; let freedom ring from Hungary to Harlem, from Palestine to Chechnya, from the snows of Kilimanjaro to the winds of Chicago. As we continue to paraphrase Reverend King, let freedom ring from Kashmir to Capetown. We need a global coalition for freedom, and not merely a global alliance against terrorism. King and Nkrumah should have worked more closely together as members of global Africa and as activists of the world.

And when this happens, and when we have allowed freedom to ring in every village and every city, in every country and every continent, we will speed up the day when all God's children — Indo-Guyanese and Afro-Guyanese, indigenous and immigrant, men and women, White and Black, Jew and Gentile, Afghan and American, Hutu and Tutsi, Palestinian and Israeli, Muslim and Christian, Hindu and Buddhist, Saint and Sinner, will be able to join hands with Nkrumah's grand vision and globalize both Martin Luther King, Jr. and Malcolm X — "Free at last, Free at last, Thank God Almighty! We are free at last!" We should go beyond the Negro spiritual, and even beyond the Triple Heritage. Yet even that powerful line needs cultural globalization.

Thank Ruhanga, Almighty, we are free at last;
Thank Jehovah, Almighty, we are free at last;
Thank Bhagwan, Almighty, we are free at last;
Thank Nyame, Almighty, we are free at last;
Thank Omuchwezi, Almighty, we are free at last;
Thank Nyogbo, Almighty, we are free at last;
Thank Ogun, Almighty. we are free at last;
Thank Mwenye ezi Mungu, we are free at last;
Thank Mawo, Almighty, we are free at last;
Thank Allahu Akbar, we are free at last;
Thank the heavens, thank the stars, we are free at last.
AMEN to one, Amen to all.

NOTES

1. For some recent discussions on globalization, *see* Mohammed A. Bamyeh, 2000: *The Ends of Globalization*, Minneapolis: University of Minnesota Press; Mark Rupert, 2000: *Ideologies of Globalization: Contending Visions of a New World Order* London and New York: Routledge; and Colin Hays and David Marsh, 2000: *Demystifying Globalization*, New York: St. Martin's Press in association with Polsis, University of Birmingham, eds.

2. Consult Kwame Nkrumah, 1970: *Consciencism: Philosophy and Ideology of Neo-colonialism* New York: Monthly Review Press, also see E. G. Addo, 1997: *Kwame Nkrumah: A Case Study of Religion and Politics in Ghana*, Lanham, MD: University Press of America, pp. 153–178.

3. This was the title of the television series (BBC /PBS); the companion volume to the series is Ali A. Mazru, 1986: *The Africans: A Triple Heritage*, Boston: Little, Brown.

4. One discussion of the Mau Mau may be found in Wunyabari O. Maloba, 1993: *Mau Mau and Kenya: An Analysis of a Peasant Revolt* Bloomington: Indiana University Press, and also consult Marshall S. Clough, 1998: *Mau Mau Memoirs: History, Memory, and Politics*, Boulder, Colo.: L. Rienner.

5. For a description of the Ghanaian route to independence, see F. M. Bourret, 1960: *Ghana: The Road to Independence*, Stanford, CA and London: Stanford University Press and Oxford University Press.

6. Bourret, *Ghana: The Road to Independence*, p. 174.

7. See, P. O. Esedebe, 1994: *Pan-Africanism: The Idea and Movement, 1776–1991*, 2nd edition, Washington, D.C: Howard University Press, pp. 167–168.

8. Consult Jon Woronoff, 1970: *Organizing African Unity* Metuchen, NJ: Scarecrow Press, pp. 36–37.

9. Cited in Anna Grimshaw, 1986: *Cricket: C. L. R. James*, London, NY: Allison & Busby, ed. p. ix.

10. *See* Clarence J. Contee, 1971: "A Critical Friendship Begins: Du Bois and Nkrumah: 1935–1945," *Crisis* Volume 78, Number 6, pp.181–185.

11. For more on African Americans in Ghana, consult Ronald W. Walters, 1993: *Pan Africanism in the African Diaspora* Detroit, MI: Wayne State University Press, pp. 95–126.

12. Relatedly, an interesting collection of essays tracing the role of African Americans in United States foreign policy may be found in Micheal L. Krenn, 1998: *The African American Voice in US Foreign Policy Since World War II*, New York and London: Garland Publishing, ed.

13. For an interesting comparison of King and Malcolm X, see James H. Cone, 1991: *Martin and Malcolm and America: A Dream or a Nightmare?* Maryknoll, NY: Orbis Books.

14. On the FBI investigation of King, see Gerald McKnight, 1998: *The Last Crusade: Martin Luther King Jr., the FBI and the Poor People's Campaign*, Boulder, CO: Westview Press.

15. *New York Times* (March 13, 1964), p.20.

16. Relatedly, see William W. Sales, Jr., 1994: *From Civil Rights to Black Liberation: Malcolm X and the Organization of Afro-American Unity*, Boston, MA: South End Press, pp. 75–90.

17. A selection of Malcolm X's evolving attitudes may be found in George Breitman, 1964: *Malcolm X Speaks*, New York: Merit Publishers, ed.

18. Details on the origins of the Klan may be found in Chester L. Quarles, 1999: *The Ku Klux Klan and Related American Racialist and Antisemitic Organizations: A History and Analysis*, Jefferson, NC and London: McFarland and Co., Inc., Publishers, pp. 27–34.

19. Consult Everette Swinney, 1987: *Suppressing the Ku Klux Klan: the Enforcement of the Reconstruction Amendments, 1870–1874*, New York and London: Garland Publishing, pp. 57–102.

20. *Ibid*, pp. 203–237.

21. *New York Times* (November 29, 2001), p.1.

22. In legal battles under way, even the courts appear to be sympathetic to the arguments proffered by the US government against releasing the names of prisoners; for one such court in NJ: see *The Washington Post* (June 13, 2002), p.15.

23. *Ibid.*

24. See the concerns raised by critics in a report in the *New York Times* (December 29, 2001), p.B7.

25. For one discussion of the issues at Nuremberg, consult Alan S. Rosenbaum, 1993: *Prosecuting Nazi War Criminals*, Boulder: Westview Press.

26. For details, see Moshe Pearlman, 1963: *The Capture and Trial of Adolf Eichmann* New York: Simon and Schuster.

27. Relatedly, see Michael W. Williams, 1990: "Nkrumah and the State of Israel," *TransAfrica Forum*, Volume 7, Number 1, pp. 39–51.

28. This was discussed on the National Public Radio program *All Things Considered*, November 9, 2001.

29. There is some concern about the legal rights that are afforded to **even U.S. citizens** who are presumed to be part of Al-Qaeda or Taliban by the Ashcroft Justice Department; see a report in *The Washington Post* (June 20, 2002), p.1; an editorial in the same publication (June 20, 2002), p. 22; and an op-ed piece by a former Marine, The Washington Post (June 25, 2002), p.19.

30. See Quarles, *The Ku Klux Klan and Related American Racialist and Anti-Semitic Organizations*, pp. 53–75.

31. For an overview of lynching, consult Philip Dray, 2002: *At the Hands of Persons Unknown: The Lynching of Black America*, New York: Random House.

32. Dray, *At the Hands of Persons Unknown*, p.422.

33. For one account of the Till tragedy, see Stephen J. Whitefield, 1988: *A Death in the Delta*, New York and London: Free Press and Collier MacMillan.

34. See Merle Miller, 1980: *Lyndon: An Oral Biography*, New York: G. P. Putnam's Sons, p.443.

35. The Byrd case is described in Dray, *At the Hands of Persons Unknown*, pp. 458–60.

36. For an optimistic view of this conference, *see* Pierre Sane, 2001: "In Defence of Durban; Racism is Back on the Agenda," *UNESCO Courier,* Volume 54, Number 10 (October), pp. 10–12, and for a critical view, see Charles Krauthammer, 2001: "Disgrace in Durban," *The Weekly Standard*, Volume 7, Number 1 (September), pp. 15–16.

37. This issue is discussed in David J. Goldberg, 1996: *To the Promised Land: A History of Zionist Thought from Its Origins to the Modern State of Israel*, London and New York: Penguin Books, pp. 83–89.

38. A full treatment of the Suez crisis can be found in a collection of essays edited by William Roger Louis and Roger Owen, 1989: *Suez 1956: The Crisis and Its Consequences*, Oxford: Clarendon.

39. This episode is recounted in Robert K. Massie, 1997: *Loosing the Bonds: The US and South Africa in the Apartheid Years*, New York: Nan A. Talese, Doubleday, p.115.

40. For a discussion on aid to Israel, see Mohammed Rabie, 1988: *The Politics of Foreign Aid: U.S. Foreign Assistance and Aid to Israel*, New York, Westport, CT, and London: Praeger.

41. See Duncan L. Clarke, 1997: "U.S. Security Assistance to Egypt and Israel: Politically Untouchable?" *Middle East Journal* Volume 51, Number 2 (Spring), pp. 200–214. Data on US aid to all countries between 1945 and 1997 may be found in United States Agency for International Development, *U.S. Overseas Loans and Grants and Assistance from International Organizations July 1, 1945 and September 30, 1997* (Washington, DC: Office of Budget, Bureau of Management, US AID, 2000).

42. A report in *The Washington Post* (January 18, 2002), p.1, indicated that the Saudis were beginning to get antsy about the U.S. presence and may ask the US to withdraw, although Secretary of State Colin Powell denied in *The Washington Post* (January 19, 2002), p. 15, that such a request had been made.

43. The Jewish attitude and history toward martyrdom is discussed in Avner Falk, 1996: *A Psychoanalytic History of the Jews*, Cranbury, NJ Farleigh Dickinson and Associated Universities Press, pp. 328–329, and pp. 467–468.

44. On martyrdom in Islam, see Chapter 2 in Rudolph Peters, 1996: *Jihad in Classical and Modern Islam: A Reader*, Princeton, NJ: Markus Wiener.

45. The Iranian Revolution in 1979 drew special attention to this aspect; consult, for instance, Donald A. Braue, 1982: "Shi'i Martyr Consciousness and the Iranian Revolution," *Encounter*, Volume 43 (Autumn), pp. 377–393.

46. Readers interested in these massacres may consult Hamo B. Vasilian, 1992: *The Armenian Genocide: A Comprehensive Bibliography and Library Resource Guide* Glendale, VA: Armenian Reference Books Co, ed.

47. See Sudarshan Kapur, 1992: *Raising Up a Prophet: The African-American Encounter with Gandhi*, Boston: Beacon Press, pp. 89–90.

48. Jomo Kenyatta, 1968: *Suffering Without Bitterness*, Nairobi and Chicago: East African Publishing House and Northwestern University Press.

49. For an overview of the transition from white rule to black rule in Zimbabwe, consult Anthony Parson, 1988: "From Southern Rhodesia to Zimbabwe, 1965–1985," *International Affairs,* Volume 9, Number 4, (November), pp. 353–361; see also Victor De Waal, 1981: *The Politics of Reconciliation: Zimbabwe's First Decade*, London and Cape Town: Hurst and David Philip.

50. Readers interested in a guide to the Biafra war may consult Zdenek Cervenka, 1981: *The Nigerian War, 1967–70: History of The War, Selected Bibliography and Documents*, Frankfurt Am Main: Bernard & Graef.

51. See the report on Nelson Mandela in the *New York Times* (March 23, 1999), p.1.

52. *New York Times* (March 23, 1999), p.6.

53. For an article recommending the African experience for the Middle East, see the op-ed piece by Mark Mathabene, "The Cycle of Revenge Can Be Broken," *New York Times* (July 5, 2002), p.21.

54. This pledge was given by Nyerere on July 20, 1964. See also *The Addis Ababa Summit 1963*, publication of the Government of Ethiopia, Ministry of Information, 1963.

55. A treatment of the two leaders' ideological variants of socialism can be found in Steven Metz, 1982: "In Lieu of Orthodoxy: The Socialist Theories of Nkrumah and Nyerere," *Journal of Modern African Studies* Volume 20, Number 3 (September), pp. 377–342.

LECTURE 3

NKRUMAHISM OUT OF THE SHADOWS

Why is this third lecture subtitled "Out of the Shadows"? It is partly because the first two lectures emphasized the shadows of globalization and counter-terrorism. But in addition, this lecture is out of the shadows and more with some of the key personalities of Africa's anti-colonial history. Africa also seeks to be out of the shadows and more with the quest for a creative African revolution.[1] Indeed, we shall examine once again how Africa seeks to be out of the shadows and in quest of an empowered and constructive role in a global order.

Africans during Nkrumah's period often revered **revolutionary presidents**; Americans, on the other hand, respect **warrior presidents**. Jomo Kenyatta was revered because his name was associated with the Mau Mau war in Kenya and with the armed struggle for independence — was that a revolution?[2]

Julius K. Nyerere of Tanzania was regarded as revolutionary partly because he became the most radical voice of Pan Africanism after the overthrow of Nkrumah. Nyerere was also regarded as a revolutionary innovator in socialism and a left-wing experimentalist — was that a revolution?[3]

Milton Obote was regarded as a revolutionary because of his **Common Man's Charter** his move to the left and his serving as a disciple to Nkrumah on the issue of **continental** African unity.[4]

All of the former Portuguese countries started independence with Marxist or neo-Marxist regimes. They had strong revolutionary credentials. **None** of the former British countries started independence with genuinely Marxist or Leninist regimes. Kwame Nkrumah described **himself** as Marxist-Leninist, but his **government** was far from that. Neither was the government of Robert Mugabe as a regime.

If **all** former Portuguese colonies started as Marxist or neo-Marxist, and none of the former British colonies did that, what about Francophone regimes? They were mixed — a few Marxist-Leninist and others deeply capitalist. Countries like Congo (Brazzaville) experimented with Leninism. Countries like the Ivory Coast explored the open market and its capitalist ideologies.

In this lecture, we shall pay special attention to African leaders who claimed revolutionary credential and were at the same time historically connected to Kwame Nkrumah. Sékou Touré was a great benefactor of Kwame Nkrumah's. When Nkrumah was overthrown, Touré invited him to Conakry. Here was a debt being graciously paid back. When Sékou Touré and his people voted against France in 1958 — thus rejecting colonialism by consent — Kwame Nkrumah made important gestures of solidarity, including funds to Guinea and the creation of the Ghana-Guinea Union.[5]

Sékou Touré in 1958 said "No" to French colonialism, but not to friendship with France. The former colonial power rejected Sékou Touré more totally.[6] Nkrumah extended a hand of support to Sékou Touré in his hour of need.

In 1966, the soldiers of Ghana and half the population rejected Kwame Nkrumah. This time, it was Sékou Touré who extended a hand of support to Kwame Nkrumah in his hour of need. Nkrumah had created the Ghana-Guinea [and later Mali] Union as a territorial expression of solidarity with Sékou Touré when Touré was thrown out in the cold by France. Sékou Touré created the Co-Presidency for Nkrumah, as a co-ruler of Guinea when Ghana threw out Nkrumah in the cold.

Touré was a fascinating triple heritage figure. Guinea was predominantly a Muslim country. Touré himself was Muslim enough to be elected Chair of the Organization of the Islamic Conference.

Touré was also neo-Marxist enough to be widely regarded as one of the tough left-wing dictators of post-colonial Africa. Nkrumah found his second post-colonial home in Touré's Guinea. Guinea was later to be also Nkrumah's first burial ground.

The story of Kwame Nkrumah and Sékou Touré as political friends needs to be written in full.[7] They were indeed political friends rather than personal buddies. But their loyalty to each other was movingly exemplary. A Francophone former trade unionist and an Anglophone who nearly became a priest forged a political friendship which, in spite of its ups and downs and its imperfections, had the magnitude of Greek drama.

If Touré helped Nkrumah to bridge the divide between Anglophone and Francophone Africa, where did Nkrumah look for other bridges? In bridging the divide between Black Africa and Arab Africa, Nkrumah found an ally also in Gamal Abdel Nasser of Egypt. Nasser even published a book entitled *The Philosophy of the Revolution* as part of his credentials as a revolutionary.[8]

In bridging the divide between armed liberation and Gandhian non-violent decolonization, Nkrumah found an ally in Jomo Kenyatta in Kenya, whom the British regarded as the founder of the Mau Mau movement.

In the debates between incremental Pan-Africanism and rapid unification, Nkrumah found a rival in Julius K. Nyerere of Tanzania.

But Nyerere was a revolutionary in other senses as well. He pushed the cultural revolution of Swahilization as a national language and national culture. He translated Shakespeare's *Julius Caesar* and *Merchant of Venice* into Kiswahili. And, he was among the first Africans to give a name to his party in an indigenous language — Chama Cha Mapenduzi [Party of the Revolution].[9]

3.1 Four Revolutionaries in African History[10]

Of the three founding fathers of Anglophone post-colonial East Africa — Kenyatta, Obote, and Nyerere–the most consistent admirer of Kwame Nkrumah was perhaps Milton Obote of Uganda.[11] In some ways, it is odd that this should be so. Nkrumah had links with Kenya's Jomo Kenyatta and Tanzania's Julius Nyerere, which were more obvious than his links with Obote. Nkrumah knew Kenyatta many years before the nationalist movement in Africa gathered momentum. He was involved with Kenyatta in organizing the historic 1945 Pan-African conference in London which brought together Africans, African Americans, and West Indians. The meeting had a more effective African component than any of the major pan-African conferences which preceded it. The preceding meetings had been more overwhelmingly led and controlled by Black people from the Americas. But the Pan-African Congress in 1945 signified the beginning of African dominance in Pan-Black movements. Jomo Kenyatta was the secretary of the Pan-African Congress in Manchester in 1945. Kwame Nkrumah was also an important participant in organizing the conference.[12] The comradeship in arms between Kenyatta and Nkrumah had, therefore, a longer standing significance than any relationship that Nkrumah ever evolved with either Obote or Nyerere, but far less profound than the friendship between Nkrumah and Sékou Touré.

There was also the link of the shared experience as "prison graduates" which bound Nkrumah and Kenyatta. Part of the mystique they acquired as nationalistic fighters was heightened by a period spent behind political bars. As symbols of Africa's fighting spirit during the colonial period, Nkrumah and Kenyatta had perhaps no equals. Nyerere's reputation came much later as a symbol of post-independence African radicalism rather than of pre-independence African militancy. Obote's international reputation was acquired mainly after independence. His achievements between 1962 and 1971 were in the field of mediation abroad and unification at home rather than in radical militancy, either nationalistic or socialistic.

Kenyatta and Nkrumah became household names among nationalists all over Africa and among their sympathizers abroad. The Mau Mau movement in Kenya associated Kenyatta with violent revolutionary insurrection against colonialism, while the techniques of "positive action" enunciated by Nkrumah associated his name with agitation and non-violent resistance in Ghana.

Nyerere's position in relation to Nkrumah was of course different from Kenyatta's. Many would argue that the torch of African radicalism, after the coup which overthrew Nkrumah in 1966, was in fact passed to Nyerere. The great voice of African self-reliance, and the most active African head of government in relation to liberation in Southern Africa from 1967 until the 1980s was in fact Julius Nyerere. Tanzania was a triple heritage country. By some estimates there are more Muslims than Christians in Tanzania. Yet, Nyerere as a revolutionary was popular figure across religions.

In reality, Nkrumah and Nyerere had already begun to be rivals as symbols of African radicalism before the coup which overthrew Nkrumah. Nkrumah was beginning to be suspicious of Nyerere in this regard. The two most important issues over which Nyerere and Nkrumah before 1966 might have been regarded as rivals for continental pre-eminence were the issues of African liberation and African unity. It was soon clear that the most difficult problems of decolonization were likely to be the Portuguese dependencies and Rhodesia. The Organization of African Unity (OAU), when it came into being in May 1963, designated Dar es Salaam as the headquarters of liberation movements. The choice was partly determined by the proximity of Dar es Salaam to Southern Africa as the last bastion of colonialism and white minority rule. But the choice was also determined by the emergence of Nyerere as an important and innovative figure in African politics.

Nkrumah's Ghana did make a bid to be the headquarters of liberation movements but Nkrumah lost the battle. If the reason had simply been that Dar es Salaam was closer to the arenas of colonial conflict, Nkrumah might have accepted this more readily. But at least as important a reason for the success of Dar es Salaam in being designated the Mecca of liberation movements was the fact that Nkrumah, by mid-1963, had already accumulated several enemies, especially in French-speaking Africa. Nkrumah's encouragement of dissidents from neighbouring countries, although it had yet to reach the proportions it reached in 1965, had begun to rear its head as a grievance among neighbours. **As the years went by, Nkrumah felt that freedom fighters were not simply those who were fighting against colonial rule but also those who were fighting against their own African neo-colonial regimes.** This was domestic revolution versus anti-colonialism of the first phase. The hospitality he extended to rebels from his French-speaking neighbours, and even to dissidents from Nigeria, made him less and less acceptable as a patron of major Pan-African ventures, especially if these depended on the blessing of the OAU. In 1963, suspicion of Nkrumah was already strong enough to make it unlikely that Accra, Ghana, would be acceptable as the official liberation capital of the African continent. Nkrumah strongly resented this reaction.

3.2 Degrees of Pan-Africanism

The other major arena in which Julius Nyerere was a rival to Nkrumah was the arena of regional integration. For years, Nkrumah had been the eloquent voice of Pan-Africanism and the symbol of the continent's quest for greater integration. On a more modest scale, Nkrumah had even attempted to lead a union first between Guinea and Ghana, and later between Guinea, Ghana and Mali. Guinea and Mali were Muslim societies; Ghana was predominantly Christian. But these triple heritage attempts at unification which Nkrumah had led proved abortive.

Then, in 1961 and 1962, it appeared as if Nyerere was going to succeed in leading the East African countries to a regional federation of Tanzania, Kenya and Uganda. By June 1963, the three heads of government in East Africa — Kenyatta, Obote, and Nyerere — felt confident enough to announce plans to form an East African federation before the end of the year. In 1960, Nyerere had already stolen the limelight on federalism in Africa by announcing his readiness to delay Tanganyika's independence until Kenya and Uganda became independent if this would facilitate the formation of an East African federation. In June 1963, Kenya was still not independent, but the other two had attained theirs. This time, the clarion call was not for Tanzania to delay its independence but for Kenya to speed up its own timetable of decolonization. The British were called upon to grant Kenya independence by December 1963 so as to enable it to join in a federation with the other two. It was in this sense that Nyerere had by that time become a symbol of African unification, apparently standing a greater chance of success in effective inter-territorial integration than Nkrumah had stood in his own ventures with Guinea and Mali.

Nkrumah's reaction was not overly subtle. He propounded a new thesis that sub-regional unification of the kind envisaged in East Africa was in fact simply "Balkanization writ large." Further, the enterprise was likely to compromise the bigger ambition of a continental union in Africa. It was a case of the good being the enemy of the best — and East Africans who accepted the minimally good achievement of sub-regional federation would no longer have the incentive to embark on continental union as a more effective bulwark against neo-colonialism and poverty. Nkrumah pointed out that his own country could not very easily join an East African federation. This proved how discriminatory and divisive the whole of Nyerere's strategy was for the African continent.

Nyerere treated Nkrumah's counter-thesis with contempt. He asserted that to argue that Africa had better remain in small bits than form bigger entities was nothing more than "an attempt to rationalize absurdity." He denounced Nkrumah's attempt to deflate the East African federation movement as petty mischief-making arising from Nkrumah's own sense of frustration in his own Pan-African ventures.

3.3 Warrior Presidents Americana

While Africans in the early decades of independence have often revered revolutionary presidents like Nkrumah and Nyerere, Americans have always saluted warrior presidents all the way from George Washington to George W. Bush.

We must, at this stage, note a fundamental point about global wars in the 20th century. World War I, World War II and the Cold War — though global in their consequences — were primarily conflicts between

Northern powers. The confrontations were either between different European powers or between the United States and the Soviet Union. Fundamentally, these were inter-Northern (or intra-Northern) conflicts.

But is George W. Bush right that the struggle against terrorism is the first war of the 21st century? Or should we view it as the first global war which is South against North [rather than North against North], with the south as the initiator? Is it also the first global conflict in which one side consists of **non-state** actors (e.g. Usama bin Laden and Al-Qaeda) and the other consists of states?

While globalization has afforded Africa a more visible role in diplomacy, it has also made Africa vulnerable when diplomacy degenerates into violence. The dates August 7, 1998 and September 11, 2001 dramatized this transition to violence.

Usama bin Laden may or may not be the man behind the atrocities committed against the United States Embassies in East Africa in August 1998 and the atrocities in America on September 11, 2001, but, he has become a symbol. It may be time to divide the passions between **Usamaphobia** (the hate or fear of Usama and what he stands for) and **Usamaphilia** (the secret admiration he definitely enjoys among the frustrated and desperate masses of those humiliated by either Israeli policies or American power and global reach).

The politics of **Usamaism** have affected me in ways of the Triple Heritage: in my capacities as a Kenyan national, as a long time African resident in America, as a Muslim and as a human being (hopefully citizen of the world). The destruction of the U.S Embassy in Nairobi on August 7, 1998 killed over two hundred Kenyans and twelve Americans — the brunt of the attack was, therefore, borne by Kenyans. Nairobi and Dar es Salaam in 1998 were ghastly dress rehearsals for New York and Washington three years later.[13]

My eldest son is a U.S. citizen working for the U.S. Federal Government in Washington, D.C. My son works for a department other than Defense, but hypothetically he might have been visiting a friend at the Pentagon. However, that morning, he happened to be at his own desk at a safe distance. He and I grieved for those who were at the Pentagon.

I am Muslim and I am Chairman of the Centre for the Study of Islam and Democracy in Washington, D.C. and a member of the Council of the Centre for Muslim-Christian Understanding at Georgetown

University, Washington D.C. I am also one of the Directors of the American Muslim Council in Washington. All the Islamic organizations to which I belong in the United States promptly distanced themselves from the atrocities on the World Trade Centre and the Pentagon. American Muslims had, ironically, voted overwhelmingly for George W. Bush in the presidential elections of November 2000.[14]

In my capacity as a citizen of the world, I have seen the phenomenon of terrorism become globalized. Innocent pedestrians on a street in Nairobi were killed in the hundreds in 1998 because a Saudi sympathizer of oppressed Iraqis and Palestinians, orchestrating world conflict from Afghanistan, held the United States responsible for the deaths of innocent children in Baghdad and Gaza. This was real international complexity. But this is also assuming Usama bin Laden was indeed responsible for the destruction of the U.S. Embassies in East Africa.

It is estimated that among the dead in the World Trade Centre in 2001 are dozens of Africans and hundreds of Muslims — ranging from Nigerian and Arab investors to Bangladeshi restaurant waiters.

But it is not just terrorism that has become globalized. It is also its causes — the frustrations and desperation of people affected by decisions made in Washington, New York, Paris, London and Moscow. A global coalition against terrorism would only make sense if it included addressing the causes of terrorism.

The single most explosive cause of anti-American terrorism is the perceived alliance between the United States and Israel against major Muslim concerns. Nkrumah saw Zionism as dangerously allied to imperialism. The world needs a coalition today more than ever to seek a permanent solution to the Middle Eastern conflict, especially the Arab-Israeli core. Palestinians and Israelis cannot solve their problems on their own. The United States is too pro-Israel to be an honest broker. We need a coalition of representatives of the European Union, the United States, the Organization of the Islamic Conference, the League of Arab States, and Russia to help the Palestinians and Israelis find a permanent solution to the problem. Without such a solution we can forget about a world without terrorism.

There was a time when the Zionist movement considered establishing a Jewish state in East Africa. At the turn of the 20th century, Joseph Chamberlain, Britain's colonial Secretary, offered Theodor Hertzel parts of what is today Kenya and Uganda. The real estate offered to the

Jews included what were later known as the White Highlands of Kenya. Fortunately for East Africa, the Zionist movement could not reach consensus. Britain's offer to the Jews was turned down.[15]

In order to recover the White Highlands, Africans in Kenya had to wage a guerrilla war, denounced by the British as terrorist.[16] The Mau Mau war nearly became a war against the **Jewish Highlands of Kenya.**

But while terrorism has since then been in the process of globalization, the concept of an "act of war" has by no means found a global standard. How many Americans would acknowledge that the Anglo-American no-fly zones imposed on Iraq for the last decade are a continuing act of war? Iraqis are not allowed to fly planes in their own air space. And yet the no-fly zones over Iraq have no United Nations authorization or legal validation.[17] Iraqis get bombed if they challenge American or British planes over Iraqi territory. African territory was bombed by President Ronald Reagan (Libya) and President Bill Clinton (Sudan).

How many members of the Bush administration would accept that the Israeli occupation of the West Bank and Gaza are what a Foreign Minister of India once described as "permanent aggression"? Indeed, are not the Israeli settlements on occupied land illegal and tantamount to belligerency? President George W. Bush's father came close to declaring them as such.[18]

Every American president since Franklin D. Roosevelt has engaged in some act of war or another. Americans still have a fascination for warrior presidents. Roosevelt was inevitably embroiled in World War II; from Harry Truman onwards the United States' military casualties have been primarily in the Third World. Truman helped to initiate the Korean War; Dwight Eisenhower ended the Korean War but started planning for the Bay of Pigs operation on Cuba; John F. Kennedy unleashed the Bay of Pigs operation and helped to initiate the Vietnam War; Lyndon Johnson escalated the Vietnam war; Richard Nixon bombed Cambodia; Gerald Ford sent the Marines in a disagreement with Cambodia over a US cargo-ship, the Mayaguez; Jimmy Carter attempted to thwart the Iranian revolution and paid heavily for it; Ronald Reagan perpetrated acts of war in Lebenon, the Caribbean, Libya and in shooting down a civilian airline in the Persian Gulf; George Bush Senior invaded Panama and is most famous for Desert Storm in the Persian Gulf; Bill Clinton let military action against Yugoslavia over Kosovo and bombed Sudan and

Afghanistan; George W. Bush has already inherited a decade of bombing Baghdad and subsidizing half a century of Israeli militarism against Palestinians. Now this younger Bush has embarked on what he once called a "crusade against terrorism"starting with bombing Afghanistan. Apart from former Yugoslavia, all casualties of U.S militarism have been in the Third World.

Every American president since Franklin Roosevelt has regarded an act of war as the equivalent of a **rite of passage**. The Commander-in-Chief has to "act presidential". His popularity dramatically rises.[19] Americans continue to love the warrior president. And yet, the United States hardly ever calls these engagements "acts of war". Even the war in Vietnam, which cost nearly sixty thousand American lives and millions of Vietnamese lives, was never officially declared by the United States.[20] America needs to find more humane rites of passage for its leaders. Why are presidents at their most popular when they find a war to fight?

Terrorism is getting globalized, but the definition of an "act of war" is not. Such a definition is still highly selective, depending upon the power of the perpetrator or the status of the victim.[21] For the immediate future, it may also depend upon making sure that Usamaphobia does not degenerate into Islamophobia.

The blood of the innocent cries out not just for a coalition against terrorism but for a coalition in search of genuine peace.

I grew up in a Kenya engulfed in a war of liberation which the British called "terrorist" — the Mau Mau war of the 1950s. I have personally met people like Nelson Mandela and Yassir Arafat, men once denounced as terrorists, but who lived to win the Nobel Prize for Peace. Some of their acts of war were in the past localized and regional. But now it is not just terrorists "who can run but cannot hide." Such a situation has become the human condition itself.

What happened at the World Trade Centre has no excuse. Even terrorism as a style of war ought to have rules. It is a pity there is no Geneva Convention laying down the rules and ethics of terrorist engagement.

For example, the terrorists could have avoided hitting the World Trade Centre at the peak hour of 9 o'clock in the morning, and attempted instead to hijack an evening flight at 9 o'clock **at night**, thus cutting down the casualty rate by three quarters. Or more ethically, the terrorists could have avoided the World Trade Centre altogether, and gone only for the Pentagon.

Just as there is sometimes honour among thieves, there ought to be restraint among terrorists. Any ethical rules of engagement would surely have regarded an attack on the World Trade Centre, at a rush hour of the day, as a dastardly act without honour or humanity.

3.4 Counter-Terrorism and the Brain Drain

September 11 may certainly be on its way towards affecting the "brain drain" from Africa as well. The nineteen dead Arabs who were accused of having blown up the World Trade Centre, the Pentagon and who hijacked the fourth plane on September 11 were all cases of the brain drain from their own countries in one degree or another.

The impact of September 11 on immigration policies in the Western world seems to be towards greater scrutiny and reduced Western hospitality.[22] There was a time when high scientific and technological qualifications were regarded as attractive credentials for immigration into the West.

The superb skills of those Arabs who apparently perpetrated the atrocities of September 11 must surely reduce the attractiveness of technical skills as qualifications for new immigration. Who would want immigrants who are clever enough to hijack and fly **four** passenger jets in one morning within the most advanced technological power in history?

There was a time in the annals of the United States when unique technical qualification were a passport to the green card. After September 11, an Arab who is "too clever by half" is more likely to be seen as a threat than as a potential asset to the society.

When he was President of Ghana, Jerry Rawlings used to worry especially about loosing too many Ghanaian doctors. I once heard him address this issue with singular passion. We were both attending the annual World Economic Forum in Davos, Switzerland. In his presentation at the conference, Rawlings got angrier and angrier as he talked about how newly-skilled doctors in countries like Ghana started packing their bags for Canada, Britain, France or the United States almost as soon as they were professionally qualified to reduce infant mortality or unsafe motherhood in their own countries. Jerry Rawlings' anger rose higher and higher as he reflected on this issue.

At question time, I congratulated the President on his passionate concern for vulnerable groups in a country like Ghana and their need for the services of qualified professionals. But I pointed out that the brain drain as a whole was caused by two sets of forces. There were the **pull-in factors** in the host countries — factors like greater freedom, wider opportunities, better rewards, and professional recognition. The **push-out factors** were in the countries being left behind — factors like lack of freedom, limited resources, restricted professional opportunities, and inadequate professional recognition.

I suggested to President Jerry Rawlings (as he then was) that the push-out forces in African countries included the policies of African governments which were often hostile to intellectuals. Bad government policies often also had the effect of damaging the economy or reducing freedom at home. I also suggested to Jerry Rawlings that there would have been fewer African doctors packing their bags to migrate to the West if African governments had been more supportive of African professionals, or more sensitive to the wider needs of their societies.

Jerry Rawlings and I continued the banter a little longer. He then invited me to Ghana on a future date to conclude our debate in a leisurely fashion.

My Davos dialogue with Jerry Rawlings occurred in 1998 — about three years before September 11, 2001. The question which arose after September 11 was whether in the aftermath the West had already begun to close its doors to new immigration from developing countries. Would there be fewer Ghanaian doctors and other professionals packing their bags in the future to migrate to the West? However inadvertently, is the aftermath of September 11 going to help Africa keep the doctors needed for infant mortality, unsafe motherhood and other health hazards? Has Usama bin Laden helped Jerry Rawlings realize his dream of arresting the brain drain, at least for a while? The answer is still in the womb of future history.

3.5 Between Revolution and Democracy

Rawlings was a revolutionary who turned democrat; Nkrumah was a democrat who turned revolutionary. Kwame Nkrumah started as a democrat and ended his political career as a dictator; Jerry Rawlings started his political career as a brutal dictator and ended it as a democrat.

There were stages in both these trends. On attainment of independence, Ghana was for awhile an open society. But Nkrumah electoral success was more vulnerable than many realized. The Convention People's Party (CPP) won only 57 per cent in the last national election in Ghana before independence. Its opponents won 43 per cent of the poll in the 99 contested constituencies. The CPP was also out-seated and out-voted in Ashanti and the North. And even after making allowances for the five unopposed seats, Nkrumah's popular support was not overwhelming — and certainly far less than that of Julius K. Nyerere in Tanganyika or Houphouët-Boigny in the Ivory Coast.

In any case, the poll in Ghana in that crucial pre-independence election represented only 50 per cent of the registered electorate, and probably something under 30 per cent of the total adult population This was **not** an avalanche vote for the CPP. The temptation to consolidate its power became great, and perhaps irresistible.

The Nkrumah regime moved towards monopoly of power with the one-party state. It also moved towards undermining the judiciary as an independent body. The CPP regime also succumbed to the temptations of preventive detention.

In his Pan-African politics, Nkrumah had a positive destiny with history. He remains a great African visionary. But in his domestic politics, he left Ghana less free than he himself had helped to make it.

He gave Ghana freedom from British colonial shackles — and then took away Ghana's freedom with new chains of his own. It is in that sense Nkrumah entered the state of Ghanaian history as a liberator — and left the state of Ghanaian history as a dictator.

The Commonwealth (former **British** Commonwealth) had Third World Secretaries-General for two decades — Ramphal of Guyana and Emeka Anyoukou of Nigeria.

Jerry Rawlings' destiny was in the reverse direction. Here was a man who first came to power in a military coup. He then returned to power in another military takeover. The style was sometimes brutal — including the phenomenon of multiple "regicides," executing former rulers of the land. Then, Jerry Rawlings came to power a third time through the ballot box. Many of his opponents and critics cried foul, but there was indeed considerable support for the man in the Ghanaian countryside. Jerry Rawlings rose to power a fourth time in absolute frequency — but the second time through the ballot box. this second electoral victory is conceded even by the opposition as a free election even if the outcome were resented by the losers. Fifthly, the man stepped down from power without changing the constitution to give him yet another term in office. Indeed, he let the electoral system be so free that his own party was defeated at the polls. Table 1 shows the six stages of Jerry Rawlings' route to democratization.

TABLE 1

The six Stages of Jerry Rawlings Route of Democratization

First   Brutal military coup of 1979.

Second   Another military takeover of 1982.

Third   Triumph through the ballot box but not acknowledged by the opposition (1992).

Fourth   Triumph through the ballot box and accepted by the opposition as free and fair (1996).[23]

Fifth   Stepping down from power without attempting to change the constitution (2000).

Sixth   Allowing the electoral system to be free enough to defeat his own party (2000).

Is it really true that Jerry Rawlings had no choice but to give up power without attempting to manipulate the system? After all, Robert Mugabe tried his best to manipulate the system in spite of sanctions from the European Union and the United States, and the threat of suspension from the Commonwealth. In Zambia, Chiluba wanted to change the Constitution for a third term as president, and was thwarted more by his own party than by Western disapproval. In Kenya, Daniel arap Moi is still keeping his people guessing about whether he would play by the rules and bow out of power at long last.

Rawlings in 2000–2002 was not Mugabe, Chiluba or Moi. He accepted the rules of the game and bowed out. Why should he not be given credit for not manipulating the system — Mugabe-style? African rulers who relinquish power voluntarily should be given credit for doing so.

We all know how tough it is to be a gracious **loser**. But in Africa it seems to be equally tough to be a gracious **winner**. Chiluba won against Kenneth Kaunda — and then proceeded to humiliate Kaunda and even seek to deprive him of his Zambian citizenship.

In Ghana in the year 2002, is it the losers who are being ungracious — or is it the winners? Is it the supporters of the old regime who are being ungracious — is it the members of the new of the dispensation?

> Fool! Said my muse to me
> Look in thin heart and ponder.

Perhaps there is a need for graciousness among both winners and losers in Ghana. In politics, good manners are sometimes almost as important as good morals.

3.6   Out of the Shadows? A Conclusion

Meanwhile globalization, when it is out of the shadows, has also permitted the emergence of Black and African moral leadership on a world scale. It began with the Nobel Prize winners for peace. Over the years, these have included Ralph Bunche (1950), Albert Luthuli (1960), Martin Luther King Jr. (1964), Anwar Sadat (1978), Desmond Tutu (1984), Nelson Mandela (1994), F. W. de Klerk (1994) and Kofi Annan (2001). Black Nobel Prize winners in literature or economics are not necessarily moral leaders.

Globalization has also witnessed the rise of Africans to positions of leadership in global organizations. But here, as I said in 2001 in my W. E. B. Du Bois lectures in Accra, it may be worth distinguishing between Africans of the soil and Africans of the blood. Boutros Boutros-Ghali, the first African Secretary-General of the United Nations, was an African of the soil. Kofi Annan, the second African Secretary-General, is an African of the blood and the soil. North Africans like Boutros-Ghali belong to the African continent (the soil) but not to the Black race (the blood). On the other hand, African Americans are Africans of the blood (the Black race) but not of the soil (the African continent). Sub-Saharan Africans like Kofi Annan are in reality both Africans of the soil (the African continent) and of the blood (the Black race). Globalization has given Africans of the soil and of the blood new opportunities for leadership at the global level.

Even before the two African Secretaries-General of the United Nations, Africa had already produced a black Director-General of UNESCO (the United Nations Educational, Scientific and Cultural Organization) in Paris. He was Amadou Mahtar M'Bow, an African of the blood and of the soil from Senegal. His openly pro-Third World policies infuriated the United States, which finally withdrew from UNESCO in 1985, followed by its compliant ally, the United Kingdom. The United Kingdom returned to UNESCO in 1997 after the sweeping victory of the Labor Party in the 1996 elections.

With regard to the United Nations itself, Africa is the only region of the world apart from Europe to have produced more than one Secretary-General for the world body. Europe has produced three Secretaries-General, African two, and the other regions of the wolrd have produced either one each or none so far.

The International Court of Justice at The Hague elected in 1994 an African of the soil for its President — Mohammed Medjauni of Algeria. The World Bank in the 1990s has had two African Vice-Presidents — Callisto Madivo, an African of the blood and the soil from Zimbabwe, and Ismail Serageldin, an African of the soil from Egypt. In 1999, Serageldin was also a serious candidate to become the first UNESCO Director-General of the new millennium.[24]

Ralph Bunche and Martin Luther King, Jr. were, of course, African American Nobel Peace Laureates and therefore Africans of the blood in our sense, but not of the soil. Anwar Sadat and F. W. de Klerk were as Peace Laureates Africans of the soil but not of the blood. Albert Luthuli, Desmond Tutu and Nelson Mandela were Africans of both the soil and the blood. All three were South Africans, as was F. W. de Klerk. But we should note that F. W. de Klerk was an "African of the soil" by adoption rather than by indigenous roots to the continent. Most North Africans, on the other hand, are indigenous to the continent, although there has been considerable racial mixture with immigrants over the centuries.

As the 20th century was coming to a close, Nelson Mandela achieved a unique status. He became the first truly universal Black moral leader in the world in his own lifetime. Martin Luther King, Jr. achieved universal status after his death. When Dr. King was alive, half of mainstream America rejected him and regarded him as a troublemaker. Mandela was fortunate to have achieved universal moral admiration without having to undergo an assassination beforehand. No other Black man in history has pulled off such a "pre-humus" accomplishment (as distinct from a posthumous elegy). In the recognition of Mandela, the human race may have taken one more step forward in the search for universalized ethical sensibilities.[25]

Mandela languished in jail for 27 of the best years of his life — ostensibly punished for acts of terrorism. He later won a Nobel Prize for Peace. Usama bin Laden is unlikely to win the Nobel Prize for Peace, but if caught and in good health he should be tried by an International Tribunal like the fate of Milosevic of Yugoslavia, rather than tried by his enemies as Nelson Mandela was.

Positive globalization needs new legal and moral standards. The shadows in Africa itself are not yet fully lifting. Poverty, underdevelopment, disease and instability are still rampant. But the shadows of Africa's role in world affairs are indeed more clearly lifting. The Secretary of State of the United States, Colin Powell, is an African of the blood and a compatriot of Martin Luther King, Jr. The Secretary-General of the United Nations, Kofi Annan, is an African of both the soil and the blood and a compatriot of Kwame Nkrumah. As for W. E. B. Du Bois, he was a compatriot of both Colin Powell (fellow African American) and a compatriot of Kwame Nkrumah (fellow Ghanaian).

To paraphrase an English poet:

Deign on global Africa
To turn thine eyes
And pause a while from surfing
To be wise.[26]

NOTES

1. For some recent discussions on Africa in the new era of globalization, see, for example, Mark Huband, *The Skull Beneath the Skin: Africa after the Cold War* (Boulder, Colo.: Westview Press, 2001) and Julius O. Ihonvbere, *Africa and the New World Order* (New York: Peter Lang, 2000).

2. One discussion of the Mau Mau may be found in Wunyabari O. Maloba, *Mau*

Mau and Kenya: An Analsis of a Peasant Revolt (Bloomington: Indiana University Press, 1993).

3. Smith, William Edgett, *We Must Run While They Walk: A Portrait of Africa's Julius Nyerere* (New York: Random House, 1971, 1972).

4. For a life of Obote, see Kenneth Ingham, *Obote: A Political Biography* (London and New York: Routledge, 1994).

5. An interesting analysis of Kwame Nkrumah — from the Third World — may be found in Anirudha Gupta, "Kwame Nkrumah: A Reassessment," *International Affairs,* Volume 12, Number 2 (India), 1973, pp. 207–221.

6. Sékou Touré's regime is scrutinized by Lansine Kaba, "Guinean Politics: A Critical Historical Overview," *Journal of Modern African Studies* Volume 15, Number 1 (March 1977), pp. 25–45.

7. For an overview of the ideologies of Nkrumah and Touré, consult W. A. E. Skurnik, ed., *African Political Thought: Lumumba, Nkrumah, Touré* (Denver: University of Denver, 1968).

8. Gamal Abdel Nasser, *The Philosophy of the Revolution,* introduction by John S. Badeau, and biographical sketch by John Gunther (Buffalo: Smith, Keynes & Marshall, 1959).

9. An assessment of the Tanzanian model of socialism is offered in Andrew Coulson, ed., *African Socialism in Practice: The Tanzanian Experience* (Nottingham: Spokesman, 1979).

10. This section and the following one are drawn from Ali A. Mazrui, "Introduction," in Opoku Agyeman, *Nkrumah's Ghana and East Africa: Pan Africanism and African Interstate Relations* (Cranbury, NJ; London; Misissauga, ON: Associated University Presses, 1992), pp. 11–25.

11. Ingham, *Obote,* p.5.

12. See A. B. Assensoh, *Kwame Nkrumah of Africa: His Formative Years and the Beginning of His Political Career, 1935–1948* (Elms Court, UK: Arthur H. Stockwell, Ltd., 1989), pp. 84–86.

13. For one report lamenting the end of the African "safe haven," see *New African, 367* (October 1998), pp. 16–17.

14. American Muslims backed Bush in several ways; for instance, in the 2000 Presidential Elections, a Muslim Political Action Committee endorsed Bush; see the *Christian Science Monitor* (November 2, 2000), p.18.

15. This issue is discussed in David J. Goldbery, *To the Promised Land: A History of Zionist Thought from its Origins to the Modern State of Israel* (London and New York: Penguin Books, 1996), pp. 83–89.

16. Consult Maloba, *Mau Mau and Kenya* and Marshall S. Clough, *Mau Mau Memoirs: History, Memory, And Politics* (Boulder, Colo.: L. Rienner, 1998).

17. The United Nations has objected to the implicit authority claimed by the United States; see the discussion in Jules Lobel and Michael Ratner, "Bypassing the Security Council: Ambiguous Authorizations to Use Force, Cease-Fires and the Iraqi Inspection Regime," *American Journal of International Law,* Vol. 93, No. 1, (Jan., 1999), p.126 and pp. 132–133.

18. An account of the Bush Sr.'s administration's attempts to oppose the settlements may be found in Donald Neff, "Settlements in U.S. Policy," *Journal of Palestine Studies,* vol. 23, No. 3. (Spring, 1994), pp. 62–63. The current Bush Jr. administration appears to be unwilling to "draw a line in the sand" on the Israeli expansion of settlements.

19. Since the beginning of the war on terrorism, George W. Bush's popularity has been in the 80 per cent range.

20. The Vietnamese numbers are controversial. One study has a lower estimate; Charles Hirschmann, Samuel Preston, Manh Loi Vu, "Vietnamese Casualties during the American War: A new Estimate," *Population And Development Review* 21, 4 (December 1995), pp. 783–812, estimates the combined Vietnamese toll as approximately one million, with a margin of error of about 175000 between 1965 and 1975; the lowest figures ia about 415,000 while Hanoi claims there were two million deaths between 1954 and 1975. In contrast, there were about 58,000 American military fatalities; see also Spencer C. Tucker, ed., *Encyclopedia of the Vietnam War,* Volume One Santa Barbara, CA: ABC-CLIO, 1998), p.106.

21. The Sharon administration in Israel is constantly attempting to liken the attacks on the U.S to the Palestinian struggle for self-determination. It is blind to the fact that their occupation and continued stalling toward Palestinian statehood strengthens the hand of Palestinian extremists who have resorted to suicide attacks.

22. The popularity of right-wing figures in Europe such as Le Pen in France, the late Pym in The Netherlands, and Haider in Austria are symptomatic of the fears of different cultures in that region, less used to immigration.

23. This was perhaps the decisive stage; see Kwamina Panford, "Election and Democratic Transition in Ghana: 1991–1996," in Jean-Germain Gros, ed., *Democratization in Late Twentieth-Century Africa: Coping with Uncertianty,*

(Westport, Conn.: Greewood Press, 1998), pp. 113–128.

24. See the report in the *New York Times* (August 18, 1999), p.8 on Serageldin's candidacy.

25. Consult the report on Nelson Mandela in the New York Times (March 23, 1999), p.1.

26. These lines are stimulated by Samuel Johnson's poem, "The Vanity of Human Wishes" (London, 1749); see J. D. Fleeman, ed., *Samuel Johnson: The Complete English Poems* (New Haven and London: Yale University Press, 1971).